# Festive Banner & C

Designs by Angie Arickx

**Size:** **Banner:** 18 inches W x 1½ inches H
(45.7cm x 3.8cm)
**Coaster:** 3⅜ inches W x 3⅜ inches H
(8.6cm x 8.6cm)
**Skill Level:** Beginner

## Materials

❏ ½ sheet clear 7-count plastic canvas
❏ Uniek Needloft plastic canvas yarn as listed in color key
❏ ⅛-inch-wide (0.3cm) Rainbow Gallery Plastic Canvas
7 metallic needlepoint yarn as listed in color key
❏ #16 tapestry needle

## Project Note

Yardages given in the color key are sufficient for stitching the banner and one coaster. If you choose to stitch more coasters, additional yarn will be needed.

## Stitching Step-by-Step

**1** Cut one coaster, four stars and one of each banner piece from plastic canvas according to graphs.

**2** Stitch pieces according to graphs, filling in uncoded areas on banner pieces and coaster with black Continental Stitches.

**3** Overcast edges according to graphs.

**4** Referring to photo, using silver metallic needlepoint yarn, stitch stars to banner tabs where indicated by blue dots on graphs, placing banners in sequence to read "HAPPY NEW YEAR."

**5** *Hangers:* Cut two 6-inch (15.2cm) pieces of silver metallic needlepoint yarn. Thread ends of one piece through one of the end stars from front to back at positions indicated by blue dots on star graph. Knot ends of metallic needlepoint yarn on back, forming a hanging loop. Repeat with remaining metallic needlepoint yarn at other end of banner.

**Banner A**
36 holes x 9 holes
Cut 1

**COLOR KEY**

| Yards | Plastic Canvas Yarn |
|---|---|
| 3 (2.7m) | ■ Bright orange #58 |
| 3 (2.7m) | □ Bright blue #60 |
| 3 (2.7m) | □ Bright green #61 |
| 3 (2.7m) | ■ Bright pink #62 |
| 3 (2.7m) | □ Bright yellow #63 |
| 3 (2.7m) | ■ Bright purple #64 |
| 12 (11m) | Uncoded areas are black #00 Continental Stitches |
| | ✦ Black #00 Overcasting |
| | **⅛-inch Metallic Needlepoint Yarn** |
| 8 (20.3m) | □ Silver #PC2 |

Color numbers given are for Uniek Needloft plastic canvas yarn and Rainbow Gallery Plastic Canvas 7 Metallic Needlepoint Yarn.

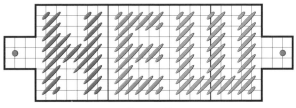

**Banner B**
28 holes x 9 holes
Cut 1

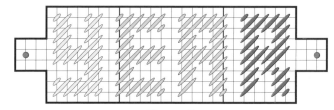

**Banner C**
30 holes x 9 holes
Cut 1

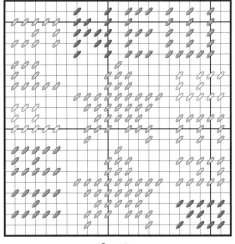

**Coaster**
22 holes x 22 holes
Cut 1

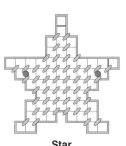

**Star**
11 holes x 11 holes
Cut 4

**COLOR KEY**

| Yards | Plastic Canvas Yarn |
|---|---|
| 3 (2.7m) | Bright orange #58 |
| 3 (2.7m) | Bright blue #60 |
| 3 (2.7m) | Bright green #61 |
| 3 (2.7m) | Bright pink #62 |
| 3 (2.7m) | Bright yellow #63 |
| 3 (2.7m) | Bright purple #64 |
| 12 (11m) | Uncoded areas are black #00 Continental Stitches |
| | Black #00 Overcasting |

**⅛-inch Metallic Needlepoint Yarn**

| | |
|---|---|
| 8 (20.3m) | Silver #PC2 |

Color numbers given are for Uniek Needloft plastic canvas yarn and Rainbow Gallery Plastic Canvas 7 Metallic Needlepoint Yarn.

# New Year's Resolution Fridgie

Design by Angie Arickx

**Size:** 4⅝ inches W x 6¾ inches H
(11.8cm x 17.1cm)
**Skill Level:** Beginner

## Materials

❑ ½ sheet clear 7-count plastic canvas
❑ Uniek Needloft plastic canvas yarn as listed in color key
❑ DMC #3 pearl cotton as listed in color key
❑ Tapestry needles: #16 and #22
❑ 3 (1-inch/2.5cm) pieces magnetic strip
❑ Hot-glue gun

## Stitching Step-by-Step

**1** Cut bear from plastic canvas according to graph.

**2** Using #16 tapestry needle, stitch piece according to graph, filling in uncoded areas on head and paws with maple Continental Stitches, and uncoded banner with white Continental Stitches.

**3** Using #22 tapestry needle and plum #3 pearl cotton, Backstitch and Straight Stitch lettering on banner.

**4** Using #16 tapestry needle, Overcast edges according to graph.

**5** Hot-glue one magnet strip to back of head. Hot-glue remaining magnet strips to back of banner at each end.

**Bear**
30 holes x 44 holes
Cut 1

**COLOR KEY**

| Yards | Plastic Canvas Yarn |
|---|---|
| 1 (0.9m) | ■ Black #00 |
| 2 (1.8m) | ☐ Beige #40 |
| 3 (2.7m) | ☐ Bright blue #60 |
| 1 (0.9m) | ▨ Bright pink #62 |
| 4 (3.7m) | Uncoded areas on head and paws are maple #13 Continental Stitches |
| 7 (6.4m) | Uncoded area on banner is white #41 Continental Stitches |
| | ╱ Maple #13 Overcasting |
| | ╱ White #41 Overcasting |
| **#3 Pearl Cotton** | |
| 2 (1.8m) | ╱ Plum #718 Backstitch and Straight Stitch |

Color numbers given are for Uniek Needloft plastic canvas yarn and DMC #3 pearl cotton.

# Hearts 'n' Stripes Mug & Coaster Set

Designs by Angie Arickx

**Size:** Mug Insert: Fits in 3¼-inch-diameter (8.2cm) acrylic mug with insert
Coaster: 3⅝ inches W x 3½ inches H (9.2cm x 8.9cm)

**Skill Level:** Beginner

## Materials

- ❏ ½ sheet Darice Super Soft clear 7-count plastic canvas
- ❏ Uniek Needloft plastic canvas yarn as listed in color key
- ❏ Coats & Clark Red Heart Classic worsted weight yarn Art. E267 as listed in color key
- ❏ #16 tapestry needle
- ❏ Plastic mug with removable interior for inserting stitched motif

## Project Note

Do not heat plastic mug, removable interior or plastic canvas insert in the microwave, as material can melt and catch fire. Use caution with hot liquids.

## Stitching Step-by-Step

**1** Cut coaster and mug insert from plastic canvas according to graphs.

**2** Stitch coaster and mug insert according to graphs.

**3** Using pink yarn throughout, Overcast coaster. Whipstitch short ends of mug insert together.

**4** Place insert inside mug, aligning seam with handle. Reposition mug interior.

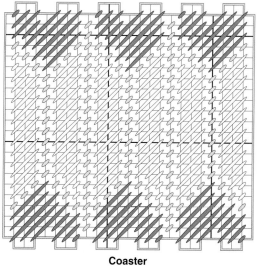

**Coaster**
24 holes x 23 holes
Cut 1

**COLOR KEY**

| Yards | Plastic Canvas Yarn |
|---|---|
| 12 (11m) | Pink #07 |
| 10 (9.1m) | Watermelon #55 |
| | **Worsted Weight Yarn** |
| 12 (11m) | White #1 |

Color numbers given are for Uniek Needloft plastic canvas yarn and Coats & Clark Red Heart Classic worsted weight yarn Art. E267.

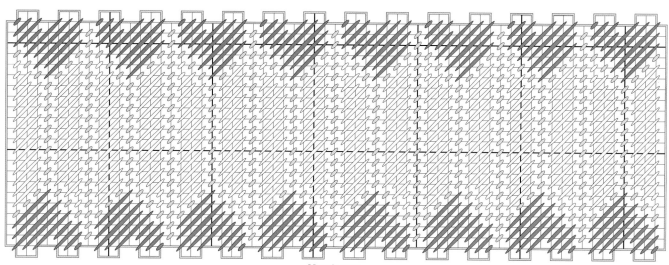

**Mug Insert**
64 holes x 23 holes
Cut 1

# Victorian Heart Potpourri Holder

Design by Ronda Bryce

**Size:** 8 inches W x 6¾ inches H x 1 inch D
(20.3cm x 17.1cm x 2.5cm)
including lace trim
**Skill Level:** Beginner

## Materials

- ❑ Small amount of 7-count plastic canvas
- ❑ 2 (6-inch/15.2cm) plastic canvas hearts from Uniek
- ❑ Worsted weight yarn as listed in color key
- ❑ White thread
- ❑ 18 inches (45.7cm) 1-inch-wide (2.5cm) white lace trim
- ❑ 12 inches (30.5cm) ¼-inch-wide (0.6cm) white satin ribbon
- ❑ 2 (1½-inch/3.8cm) white ribbon rosettes with pearl centers from Offray
- ❑ 46 (4mm) white pearl beads
- ❑ Fragrant sachet or dried potpourri
- ❑ #16 tapestry needle
- ❑ Sewing needle

## Stitching Step-by-Step

**1** Cut two holder sides from plastic canvas according to graph.

**2** Stitch sides and one heart for holder front according to graphs, filling in uncoded areas on holder front with crimson Continental Stitches. Holder back will remain unstitched except for Overcasting.

**3** Using wine yarn, Overcast holder front *and back* over curved edges, from dot to dot.

**4** Using sewing needle and white thread through step 5, stitch pearl beads to holder front according to graph.

**5** Referring to photo, stitch ribbon roses to holder front. Stitch lace to backside of holder front along rounded edges.

**6** Using wine yarn and taking two stitches per hole throughout, Whipstitch long edges of sides to straight edges of holder front and back. Whipstitch ends of sides together where they meet at bottom of heart. Overcast remaining edges.

**7** *Hanger:* Thread ends of white satin ribbon through holes on holder *back* where indicated by red dots on graph. Tie ribbon ends in a knot.

**8** Tuck sachet or potpourri into heart pocket.

| COLOR KEY | |
|---|---|
| **Yards** | **Worsted Weight Yarn** |
| 13 (11.9m) | ■ Crimson |
| 12 (11m) | ■ Wine |
| 4 (3.6m) | ☐ White |
| | Uncoded areas are crimson Continental Stitches |
| | ○ Attach pearl beads |
| | ● Attach white satin ribbon |

**Holder Side**
5 holes x 24 holes
Cut 2

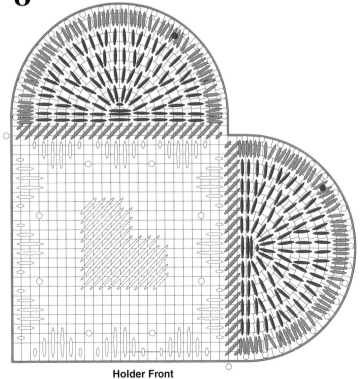

**Holder Front**
Stitch 1

# Shamrock Pin

Design by Linda Wyszynski

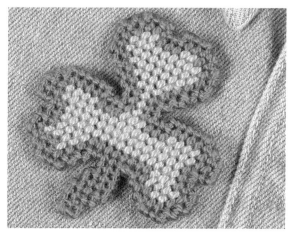

**Size:** 2¼ inches W x 2⅜ inches H (5.7cm x 6cm)
**Skill Level:** Beginner

## Materials

❑ Small amount of clear 10-count plastic canvas
❑ DMC #3 pearl cotton as listed in color key
❑ #22 tapestry needle
❑ 1-inch pin back
❑ Hot-glue gun

## Stitching Step-by-Step

**1** Cut shamrock from plastic canvas according to graph.

**2** Stitch shamrock according to graph. Using very dark emerald green, Overcast edges.

**3** Center and hot-glue pin back to back of shamrock.

### COLOR KEY

| Yards | #3 Pearl Cotton |
|---|---|
| 3 (2.7m) | ■ Very dark emerald green #909 |
| 2 (1.8m) | ☐ Medium Nile green #913 |

Color numbers given are for DMC #3 pearl cotton.

**Shamrock Pin**
22 holes x 23 holes
Cut 1

# Easter Magnets

Designs by Victoria Bailey

**Size:** Each magnet measures approximately
2 inches W x 2 inches H (5.1cm x 5.1cm)
**Skill Level:** Beginner

## Materials

❑ ½ sheet clear 10-count plastic canvas
❑ #3 pearl cotton as listed in color key
❑ 3 (9-inch/22.9cm) pieces ½-inch-wide (0.3cm)
pink satin ribbon
❑ Wiggle eyes:
      2 (7mm)
      1 (5mm)
❑ 5mm pink pompom
❑ 5 (¾-inch/19mm) artificial flowers
❑ 5 (⅝-inch/16mm) round magnets
❑ #16 tapestry needle
❑ Hot-glue gun

## Stitching Step-by-Step

**1** Cut one shape for each magnet from plastic canvas according to graphs.

**2** Using 1 strand #3 pearl cotton, stitch plastic canvas according to graphs; using adjacent colors, Overcast edges.

**3** When background stitching is complete, work embroidery:

*Basket:* Using brown, Straight Stitch basket weave.

*Egg A:* Using light green, Backstitch and Straight Stitch leaves and stems. Using light yellow, work French Knot flowers.

*Egg B:* Using light green, Straight Stitch leaves.

**4** Referring to photo throughout, embellis[h] follows:

*Large rabbit:* Wrap one piece of pink ribbon [around] ear; knot. Hot-glue one flower and 7mm eye[s] face.

*Small rabbit:* Wrap one piece of pink ribbon around neck; knot. Hot-glue one flower, 5mm eye and pompom tail to rabbit.

*Basket:* Tie remaining ribbon in a bow. Hot-glue bow and remaining flowers to basket.

**5** Hot-glue a magnet to the back of each stitched piece.

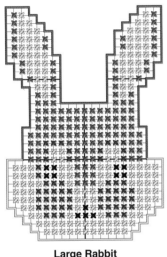

**Large Rabbit**
20 holes x 29 holes
Cut 1

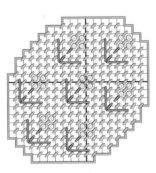

**Egg A**
18 holes x 18 holes
Cut 1

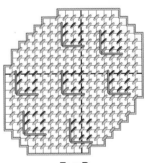

**Egg B**
18 holes x 18 holes
Cut 1

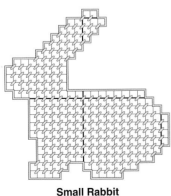

**Small Rabbit**
21 holes x 21 holes
Cut 1

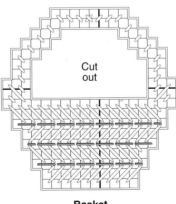

**Basket**
18 holes x 18 holes
Cut 1

**COLOR KEY**

| Yards | #3 Pearl Cotton |
|---|---|
| 7 (6.4m) | ☐ White |
| 6 (5.5m) | ■ Brown |
| 5 (4.6m) | ▨ Burgundy |
| 5 (4.6m) | ▨ Ecru |
| 5 (4.6m) | ☐ Gold |
| 3 (2.7m) | ■ Dark pink |
| 2 (1.8m) | ▨ Pink |
| 1 (0.9m) | ■ Black |
| | ✎ Brown Straight Stitch |
| 2 (1.8m) | ✎ Light green Backstitch and Straight Stitch |
| 2 (1.8m) | ○ Light yellow French Knot (1 wrap) |

# Baby Bunny Basket

Design by Vicki Blizzard

**Size:** 5¾ inches W x 7⅜ inches H x 5¾ inches D
excluding bunny and flowers
(14.6cm x 18.7cm x 14.6cm)

**Skill Level:** Beginner

## Materials

- ❏ Uniek Quick-Count 7-count plastic canvas:
    2 sheets clear
    ½ sheet pastel blue
- ❏ Uniek Needloft plastic canvas yarn as listed in color key
- ❏ #16 tapestry needle
- ❏ 8mm round black cabochon from The Beadery

- ❏ Pompoms:
    6 (½-inch/0.6mm) light pink
    6 (½-inch/0.6mm) yellow
    1 (1-inch/2.5cm) white
- ❏ 15 inches (38.1cm) 1-inch-wide (2.5cm) light pink double-faced satin ribbon
- ❏ Hot-glue gun

## Stitching Step-by-Step

**1** Cut bunny body, ear, both legs, 12 flowers, basket handle and four basket sides from clear plastic canvas according to graphs. Also cut one piece 37 holes x 37 holes from pastel blue plastic canvas for basket bottom.

**2** Stitch all clear plastic canvas pieces according to graphs, substituting yellow yarn for the pink on six of the flowers. Basket bottom will remain unstitched.

**3** Using adjacent colors, Overcast edges of flowers, legs and body. Using camel, Overcast ear. Using moss, Overcast handle.

**4** Using moss throughout, Whipstitch basket sides together at corners; Whipstitch assembled sides to unstitched basket bottom. Overcast top edge.

**5** Hot-glue yellow pompom in the center of each pink flower and pink pompom in the center of each yellow flower.

**6** Referring to photo throughout, hot-glue legs to body. Hot-glue ear to head. Hot-glue cabochon to face for eye. Hot-glue white pompom to body for tail.

**7** Hot-glue bunny to front of basket. Hot-glue ends of basket handle to right sides of basket sides. Hot-glue pink flower to handle and yellow flower to basket front beside bunny. Hot-glue remaining flowers in clusters to basket sides and back.

**8** Tie ribbon in a bow; trim ends. Hot-glue bow to bunny's neck.

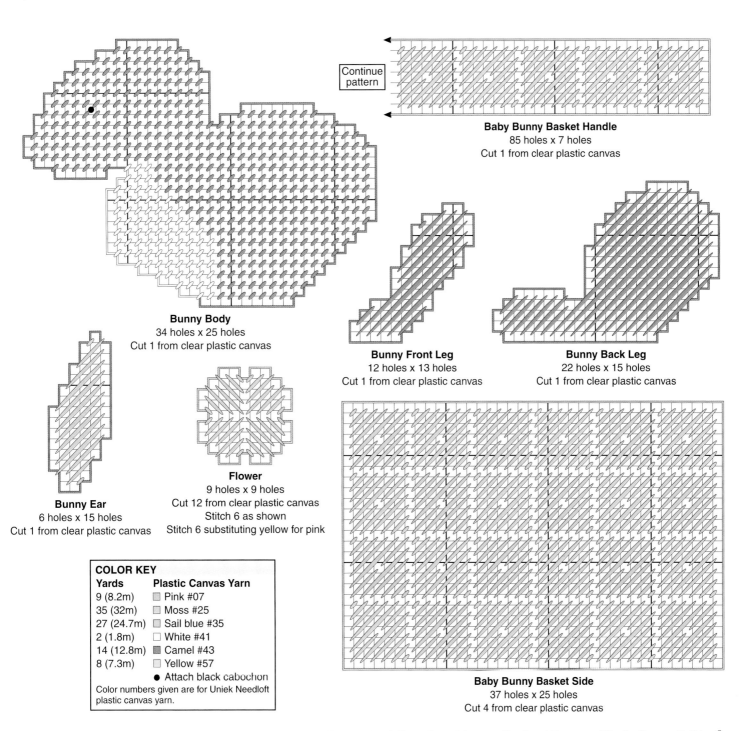

Continue pattern

**Baby Bunny Basket Handle**
85 holes x 7 holes
Cut 1 from clear plastic canvas

**Bunny Body**
34 holes x 25 holes
Cut 1 from clear plastic canvas

**Bunny Front Leg**
12 holes x 13 holes
Cut 1 from clear plastic canvas

**Bunny Back Leg**
22 holes x 15 holes
Cut 1 from clear plastic canvas

**Bunny Ear**
6 holes x 15 holes
Cut 1 from clear plastic canvas

**Flower**
9 holes x 9 holes
Cut 12 from clear plastic canvas
Stitch 6 as shown
Stitch 6 substituting yellow for pink

**COLOR KEY**

| Yards | Plastic Canvas Yarn |
|---|---|
| 9 (8.2m) | □ Pink #07 |
| 35 (32m) | □ Moss #25 |
| 27 (24.7m) | □ Sail blue #35 |
| 2 (1.8m) | □ White #41 |
| 14 (12.8m) | ■ Camel #43 |
| 8 (7.3m) | □ Yellow #57 |
| | ● Attach black cabochon |

Color numbers given are for Uniek Needloft plastic canvas yarn.

**Baby Bunny Basket Side**
37 holes x 25 holes
Cut 4 from clear plastic canvas

# Bunny Bookmark

Design by Judi Kauffman

**Size:** 1⅛ inches W x 3 inches H excluding ribbon (2.9cm x 7.6cm)

**Skill Level:** Beginner

## Materials

- ❑ Small amount of clear 14-count plastic canvas
- ❑ DMC 6-strand cotton embroidery floss as listed in color key
- ❑ 9 inches (22.9cm) 1-inch-wide (2.5cm) yellow grosgrain ribbon
- ❑ Small amount of off-white felt (optional)
- ❑ #22 tapestry needle
- ❑ Seam sealant
- ❑ Tacky craft glue

## Project Note

Continental Stitches are worked using 6 strands embroidery floss. Cut a length of floss 18–24 inches (45.7–61cm). Separate all 6 strands of floss, then recombine without twisting before threading needle.

## Stitching Step-by-Step

**1** Cut bookmark from plastic canvas according to graph.

**2** Using 6 strands cotton embroidery floss, stitch bookmark according to graph, filling in uncoded areas with ecru Continental Stitches.

**3** When background stitching is complete, work French Knot nose with 6 strands medium cranberry floss. Using medium baby blue embroidery floss throughout, Straight Stitch whiskers with 1 strand; Backstitch ears with 2 strands; work French Knot eyes with 6 strands. *Do not Overcast edges.*

**4** Glue one end of yellow 1-inch-wide (2.5cm) grosgrain ribbon to wrong side of bunny's ears; let glue dry completely. Treat ends of grosgrain ribbon with seam sealant.

**5** *Optional felt backing:* Using bunny as a template, cut off-white felt to fit on back of bunny. Glue felt to back of bunny, covering end of ribbon.

### COLOR KEY

| Yards | 6-Strand Embroidery Floss |
|---|---|
| 1 (0.9m) | ■ Medium cranberry #602 |
| 1 (0.9m) | ☐ Very light cranberry #605 |
| 5 (4.6m) | Uncoded areas are Ecru Continental Stitches |
| 1 (0.9m) | ╱ Medium baby blue #334 1-strand Straight Stitch |
| | ╱ Medium baby blue #334 2-strand Backstitch |
| 1 (0.9m) | ● Medium cranberry #602 6-strand French Knot |
| | ● Medium baby blue #334 6-strand French Knot |

Color numbers given are for DMC 6-strand cotton embroidery floss.

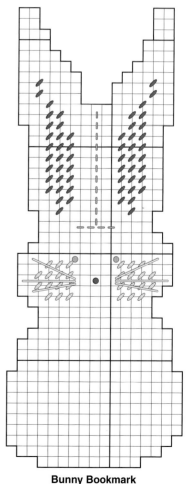

**Bunny Bookmark**
17 holes x 43 holes
Cut 1

# Easter Egg Animals

Designs by Janelle Giese

**Sizes:** **Bunny:** 2¾ inches W x 3¼ inches H x
4 inches D (7cm x 8.2cm x 10.2cm)
**Duck:** 2¾ inches W x 2⅝ inches H x
3¾ inches D (7cm x 6cm x 9.5cm)

**Skill Level:** Beginner

## Materials

- ❑ ⅔ sheet clear 7-count plastic canvas
- ❑ Chenille yarn as listed in color key
- ❑ DMC #8 pearl cotton as listed in color key
- ❑ #16 tapestry needle
- ❑ Hot-glue gun

## Stitching Step-by-Step

### Bunny

**1** Cut bunny head, base and egg cup side from plastic canvas according to graphs.

**2** Stitch bunny head and base according to graphs. Bend egg cup side into a ring, overlapping ends by two holes; stitch ring according to graph.

**3** Using white, Overcast all but the bottom edges of head; Overcast one edge of egg cup side for top.

**4** Using black #8 pearl cotton, work Backstitch and Straight Stitch on bunny head and base, passing over each eye six times. Using 2 strands natural yarn, Straight Stitch bunny's nose.

**5** Using white chenille yarn throughout, Whipstitch bottom edge of head to base where indicated by blue line on graph.

**6** Whipstitch bottom of egg cup side to unstitched area on base, positioning overlap behind bunny's head. *Note: There will be one unstitched bar between head and side of egg cup on base.* Hot-glue head to egg cup side.

**7** *Tail:* Wrap 1 yard (0.9m) of white chenille yarn around two fingers. Tie a separate strand of yarn around center, knotting tightly. Do not trim tails of tied strand. Clip loops; separate strand into a pompom. Thread tails of center tie through holes on back of egg cup; knot to secure.

### Duck

**1** Cut duck head, duck tail, base and egg cup side from plastic canvas according to graphs.

**2** Stitch head, tail and base according to graphs. Bend egg cup side into a ring, overlapping ends by two holes; stitch ring according to graph, substituting yellow chenille yarn for white.

**3** Using yellow, Overcast all but the bottom edges of head and tail; Overcast one edge of egg cup side for top.

**4** Using black #8 pearl cotton, work Backstitch and Straight Stitch on head and base, passing over each eye six times.

**5** Using yellow chenille yarn throughout, Whipstitch bottom edge of head to base where indicated by blue line on graph.

**6** Whipstitch bottom of egg cup side to unstitched area on base, positioning overlap behind duck's head. *Note: There will be one unstitched bar between head and side of egg cup on base.* Hot-glue head to egg cup side.

**7** Whipstitch duck tail to egg cup side and base where indicated on graph.

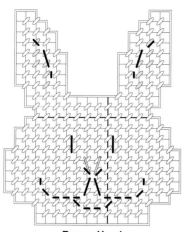

**Bunny Head**
17 holes x 20 holes
Cut 1

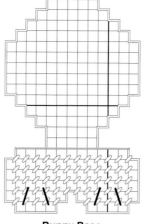

**Bunny Base**
13 holes x 20 holes
Cut 1

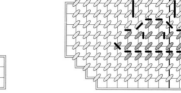

**Egg Cup Side**
42 holes x 5 holes
Cut 2
Stitch 1 as graphed for bunny
Stitch 1, substituting yellow for white, for duck

COLOR KEY

| Yards | Chenille Yarn |
|---|---|
| 12 (11m) | ☐ White |
| 1 (0.9m) | ☐ Natural |
| 3 (2.7m) | ▨ Orange |
| 9 (8.2m) | ☐ Yellow |
| | ╱ Natural Straight Stitch |
| **#8 Pearl Cotton** | |
| 2 (1.8m) | ╱ Black #310 Backstitch and Straight Stitch |

Color number given is for DMC #8 pearl cotton.

**Duck Tail**
5 holes x 5 holes
Cut 1

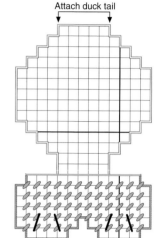

**Duck Head**
17 holes x 16 holes
Cut 1

Attach duck tail

**Duck Base**
13 holes x 20 holes
Cut 1

# Easter Bunny Holiday Holder

Design by Debbie Tabor

**Size:** 7½ inches W x 12 inches H x 6 inches D
(19cm x 30.5cm x 15.2cm)

**Skill Level:** Intermediate

## Materials

❑ 2½ sheets clear 7-count plastic canvas
❑ Uniek Needloft plastic canvas yarn as listed in color key
❑ 6-strand cotton embroidery floss as listed in color key
❑ #16 tapestry needle
❑ Hot-glue gun

## Stitching Step-by-Step

### Cutting & Stitching

**1** Cut one body, two paws, one basket base and one basket from plastic canvas according to graphs.

**2** Stitch body, paws and basket with yarn according to graphs, reversing one paw before stitching and filling in uncoded areas on body and paws with eggshell Continental Stitches. Basket base will remain unstitched. Leave pink lines on bunny body unstitched; basket will be Whipstitched to bunny along these lines during assembly.

**3** When background stitching is complete, using 6 strands white embroidery floss, work French Knot highlights in bunny's eyes, wrapping floss twice around needle. Using 6 strands black embroidery floss, Backstitch and Straight Stitch remaining details on bunny and crack in top of basket "eggs."

**4** Overcast top edge of basket between blue dots using baby blue.

### Assembly

**1** Using white yarn throughout, Overcast edges of bunny paws, leaving areas between arrows unstitched. Whipstitch tops of paws between arrows to shoulders of bunny between arrows.

**2** Shape basket by gently bending in bottoms of Easter eggs so that green dots meet; using adjacent colors, Whipstitch curved edges together.

**3** Using white yarn, Whipstitch basket side edges to body where indicated by pink lines on body graph. Using lilac yarn, Whipstitch basket base to bottom of basket and to bottom edge of body between arrows.

**4** Overcast all remaining edges of bunny using adjacent colors.

**5** Referring to photograph, using white yarn, stitch paws to basket.

| COLOR KEY | |
|---|---|
| **Yards** | **Plastic Canvas Yarn** |
| 1 (0.9m) | ■ Black #00 |
| 2 (1.8m) | ▨ Pink #07 |
| 11 (10m) | ▢ Baby blue #36 |
| 2 (1.8m) | ▢ White #41 |
| 9 (8.2m) | ▨ Lilac #45 |
| 1 (0.9m) | ▨ Turquoise #54 |
| 4 (3.7m) | ▨ Watermelon #55 |
| 6 (5.5m) | ▨ Bright orange #58 |
| 7 (6.4m) | ▢ Bright green #61 |
| 8 (7.3m) | ▨ Bright pink #62 |
| 44 (40.2m) | Uncoded areas are eggshell #39 Continental Stitches |
| | ⁄ Eggshell #39 Overcasting and Whipstitching |
| | **6-Strand Embroidery Floss** |
| 6 (5.5m) | ⁄ Black Backstitch |
| 1 (0.9m) | ⁄ White Backstitch |
| | ○ White French Knot (2 wraps) |

Color numbers given are for Uniek Needloft plastic canvas yarn.

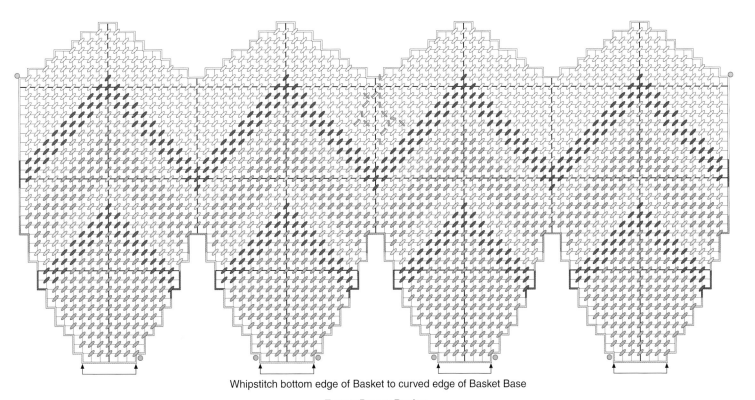

Whipstitch bottom edge of Basket to curved edge of Basket Base

**Easter Bunny Basket**
80 holes x 37 holes
Cut 1

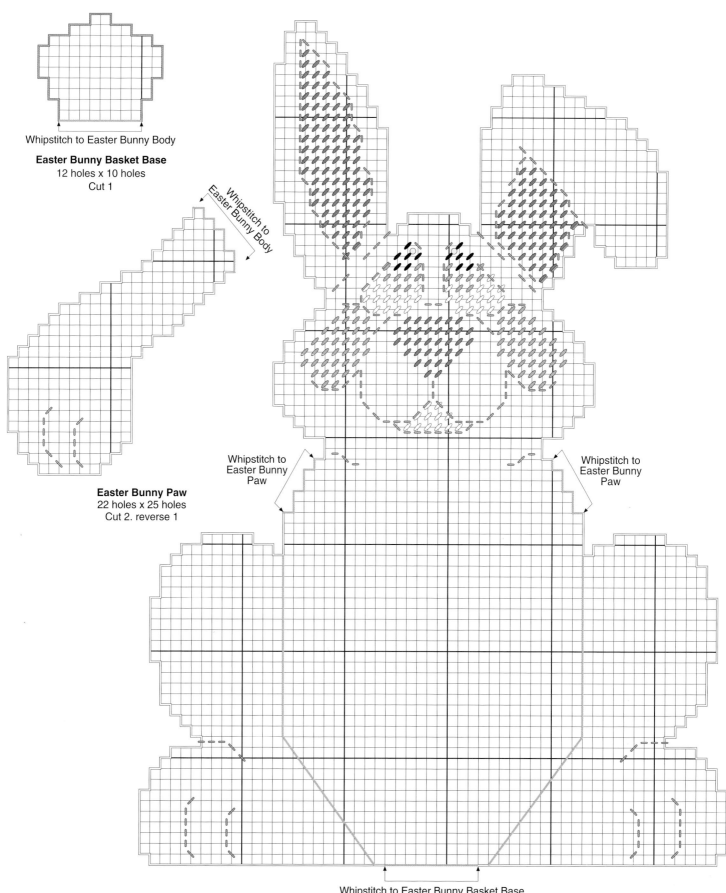

Whipstitch to Easter Bunny Body

**Easter Bunny Basket Base**
12 holes x 10 holes
Cut 1

Whipstitch to Easter Bunny Body

**Easter Bunny Paw**
22 holes x 25 holes
Cut 2, reverse 1

Whipstitch to Easter Bunny Paw

Whipstitch to Easter Bunny Paw

Whipstitch to Easter Bunny Basket Base

**Easter Bunny Body**
57 holes x 79 holes
Cut 1

# Devotional Cross

Design by Vicki Blizzard

**Size:** 13 inches W x 17 inches H (33cm x 43.2cm)
**Skill Level:** Beginner

## Materials

- ❑ 2 artist-size sheets (21⅝ x 13⅝ inches/54.9cm x 34.6cm) Uniek QuickCount clear 7-count stiff plastic canvas
- ❑ 1 sheet Uniek QuickCount clear 7-count plastic canvas
- ❑ Coats & Clark Red Heart Classic worsted weight yarn Art. E267 as listed in color key
- ❑ Uniek Needloft metallic craft cord as listed in color key
- ❑ Clear monofilament thread
- ❑ 55 (3mm) round gold beads from The Beadery
- ❑ Sawtooth hanger
- ❑ #16 tapestry needle
- ❑ Sewing needle
- ❑ Hot-glue gun

## Stitching Step-by-Step

**1** Cut two crosses and one banner from stiff plastic canvas according to graphs. Cut five small flowers, 10 large flowers, seven leaves, and letters—two L's and E's, and one each T, H, Y, W, I, B, D, O and N—from regular plastic canvas according to graphs.

**2** Stitch plastic canvas pieces according to graphs, leaving one cross unstitched for back, and Overcasting letters with gold metallic cord as you stitch.

**3** Using gold metallic cord, Whipstitch stitched cross to unstitched cross, and Overcast banner. Using forest green, Overcast leaves. Using purple, Overcast flowers.

**4** Using sewing needle and clear monofilament thread, stitch gold beads to flowers where indicated on graphs.

**5** Referring to photo throughout, hot-glue letters to banner to spell "THY WILL BE DONE." Center and hot-glue banner to crossbar. Hot-glue leaves and large flowers to cross, gluing two leaves and three flowers at top of banner; three leaves and three flowers at bottom; and one leaf and two flowers on each side. Hot-glue small flowers in circle at top of cross.

**6** Center and stitch or hot-glue sawtooth hanger to back of cross near top.

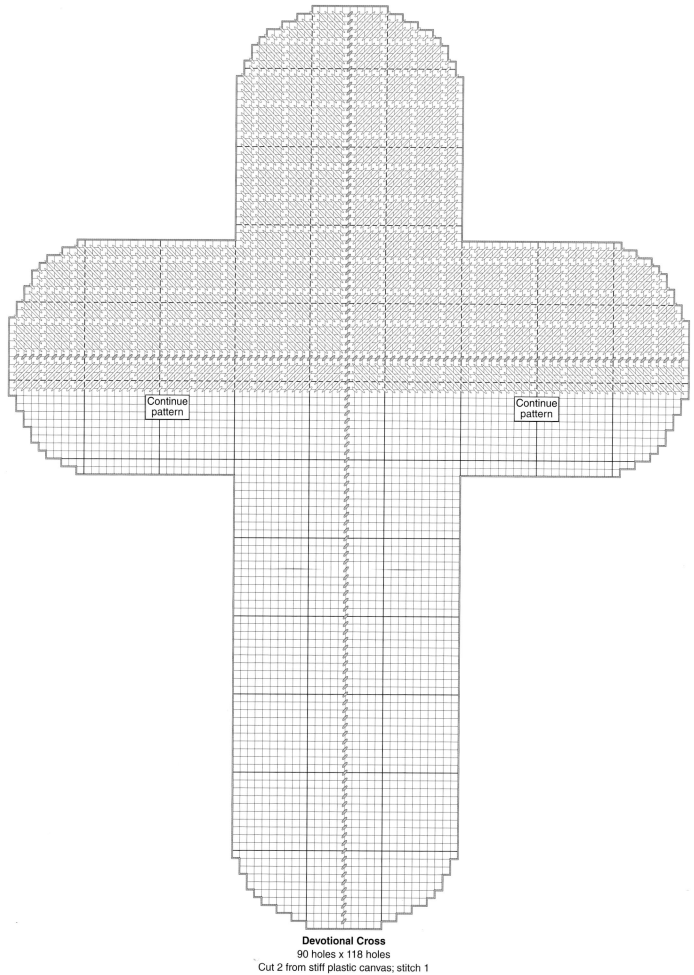

**Devotional Cross**
90 holes x 118 holes
Cut 2 from stiff plastic canvas; stitch 1

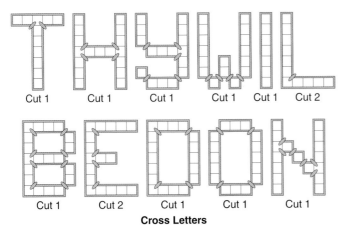

Cut 1    Cut 1    Cut 1    Cut 1    Cut 1    Cut 2

Cut 1    Cut 2    Cut 1    Cut 1    Cut 1

**Cross Letters**
All letters except "I" are 5 holes x 7 holes
Cut from regular plastic canvas

**COLOR KEY**

| Yards | Worsted Weight Yarn |
|---|---|
| 80 (73.2m) | ☐ White #1 |
| 15 (13.7m) | ■ Purple #596 |
| 15 (13.7m) | ▨ Forest green #689 |
| | **Metallic Craft Cord** |
| 20 (18.3m) | ▨ Gold #01 |
| | ● Attach 3mm gold bead |

Color numbers given are for Red Heart
Classic worsted weight yarn Art. E267 from
Coats & Clark and Uniek Needloft metallic
craft cord.

**Cross Small Flower**
3 holes x 3 holes
Cut 5 from regular plastic canvas

**Cross Large Flower**
9 holes x 9 holes
Cut 10 from regular plastic canvas

**Cross Leaf**
15 holes x 14 holes
Cut 7 from regular plastic canvas

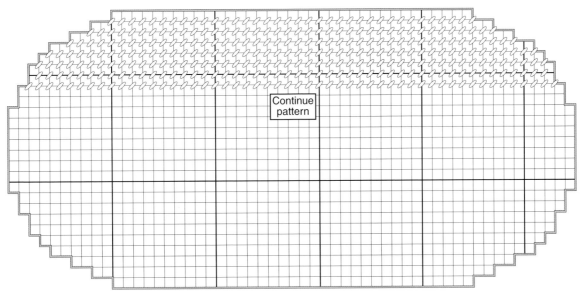

Continue pattern

**Cross Banner**
55 holes x 26 holes
Cut 1 from stiff plastic canvas

# Easter Cross Ornaments

Designs by Angie Arickx

**Size:** 2⅝ inches x 4⅞ inches H (6.7cm x 12.4cm)
**Skill Level:** Beginner

## Materials

- ½ sheet clear 7-count plastic canvas
- Uniek Needloft plastic canvas yarn as listed in color key
- Uniek Needloft iridescent craft cord as listed in color key
- #16 tapestry needle
- Sewing needle

## Stitching Step-by-Step

**1** Cut crosses from plastic canvas according to graphs.

**2** Using yarn and craft cord, stitch crosses according to graphs.

**3** When background stitching is complete, using iridescent craft cord, Backstitch, Straight Stitch and work French Knots on crosses according to graphs.

**4** Using iridescent craft cord throughout, Overcast edges.

**5** *Hanger:* Referring to diagram (page 19), work a Lark's Head Knot with craft cord in the top center hole of each cross. Knot ends of cord together.

**Pink Cross**
19 holes x 33 holes
Cut 1

**Lilac Cross**
19 holes x 33 holes
Cut 1

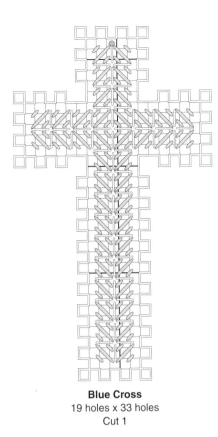

**Blue Cross**
19 holes x 33 holes
Cut 1

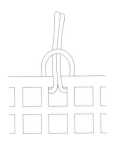

**Lark's Head Knot**

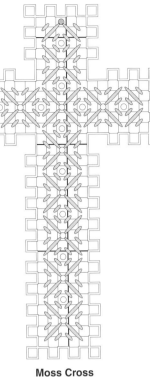

**Moss Cross**
19 holes x 33 holes
Cut 1

| COLOR KEY | | |
|---|---|---|
| **Yards** | **Plastic Canvas Yarn** | |
| 3 (2.7m) | ☐ | Pink #07 |
| 3 (2.7m) | ☐ | Moss #25 |
| 3 (2.7m) | ☐ | Sail blue #35 |
| 2 (1.8m) | ▨ | Lilac #45 |
| | **Iridescent Craft Cord** | |
| 18 (16.6m) | ☐ | White #33 |
| | ╱ | White #33 Backstitch and Straight Stitch |
| | ○ | White #33 French Knot |
| | ● | Lark's Head Knot |

Color numbers given are for Uniek Needloft plastic canvas yarn and iridescent craft cord.

# Stars & Stripes Picnic Set

Designs by Vicki Blizzard

***Size:*** **Caddy:** 7½ inches W x 8½ inches H x 5 inches D (19cm x 21.6cm x 12.7cm)
**Weights:** 4 inches W x 4 inches H (10.2cm x 10.2cm)

***Skill Level:*** Beginner

## Materials

❑ Uniek QuickCount 7-count plastic canvas:
  2 sheets stiff
  1 sheet clear regular
  ½ sheet white
❑ 3 Uniek plastic canvas stars
❑ Uniek Needloft plastic canvas yarn as listed in color key
❑ Uniek Needloft metallic craft cord as listed in color key
❑ #16 tapestry needle
❑ 2 sheets white felt
❑ 13 (3mm) round gold beads from The Beadery
❑ Sewing needle and clear thread
❑ 8-ounce package plastic doll pellets
❑ Hot-glue gun

## Stitching Step-by-Step

### Caddy

**1** Cut away gray areas from two plastic canvas stars according to graph for caddy star. Cut two caddy long sides and two caddy short sides from stiff plastic canvas, according to graphs. Cut one caddy handle from regular plastic canvas, according to graph.

**2** Cut also one piece 54 holes x 35 holes from stiff plastic canvas for caddy bottom; and one piece 52 holes x 33 holes, and two pieces 17 holes x 33 holes from white plastic canvas for dividers. Caddy bottom and dividers will remain unstitched.

**3** Stitch caddy stars, caddy sides and handle according to graphs. Using solid gold craft cord, Overcast stars and handle.

**4** Using sewing needle and clear thread, stitch gold beads to centers of stars, according to graph.

**5** Using stitched caddy sides and handle as templates, cut matching pieces from white felt, trimming the felt slightly smaller so that it will not obscure holes for Whipstitching and Overcasting when glued to back of plastic canvas. Hot-glue felt to back of each piece, making sure holes along edges remain open.

**6** Using solid gold craft cord, Whipstitch caddy sides together along corners; Whipstitch bottom to assembled sides. Overcast top edges.

**7** *Divider insert:* Using dark royal yarn throughout, Whipstitch one small divider to 17th bar from left end of large divider strip. Whipstitch remaining small divider to same side of large strip, at 17th bar from right end. (There should be 17 bars between small dividers.)

**8** Position divider in caddy. Center and tack in place on bottom. Hot-glue tops of dividers to felt lining.

**9** Center and hot-glue ends of handles to short sides of caddy on outside. Center and hot-glue a star over the handle end on each short side.

### Weights

**1** Cut away gray areas from plastic canvas star according to graph for weight star. Cut two striped weight pieces and two dark royal weight pieces from regular plastic canvas, according to graphs.

**2** Stitch star and two weight pieces according to graphs, leaving two weight pieces unstitched for backs. Using solid gold craft cord, Overcast star.

**3** Using sewing needle and clear thread, stitch gold bead to center of star, according to graph.

**4** Using solid gold craft cord, Whipstitch striped weight front to unstitched back, filling weight with half the plastic pellets before closing. Repeat with pieces for dark royal weight; center and hot-glue star to dark royal weight.

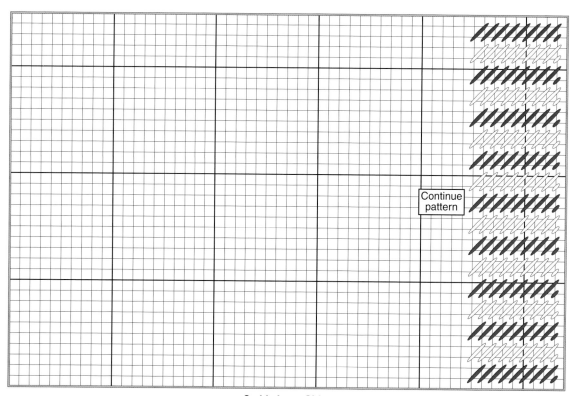

Continue pattern

**Caddy Long Side**
54 holes x 35 holes
Cut 2 from stiff plastic canvas

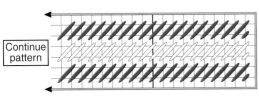

**Caddy Handle**
90 holes x 7 holes
Cut 1 from clear regular plastic canvas

**COLOR KEY**

| Yards | Plastic Canvas Yarn |
|-------|---------------------|
| 32 (29.3m) | ■ Christmas red #02 |
| 34 (32m) | □ White #41 |
| 58 (53m) | ▨ Dark royal #48 |
| **Metallic Craft Cord** | |
| 13 (11.9m) | ╱ Solid gold #20 Overcasting |
| | ● Attach gold bead |

Color numbers given are for Uniek Needloft
plastic canvas yarn and metallic craft cord.

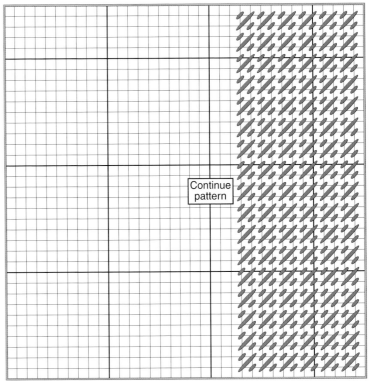

**Caddy Short Side**
35 holes x 35 holes
Cut 2 from stiff plastic canvas

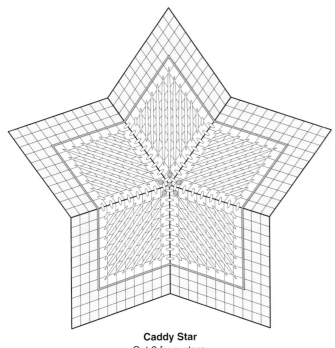

**Caddy Star**
Cut 2 from stars,
cutting away gray areas

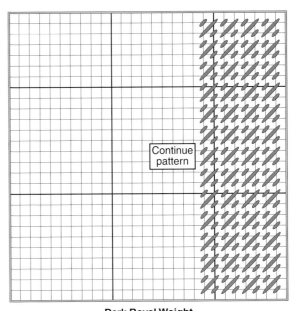

**Dark Royal Weight**
27 holes x 27 holes
Cut 2 from clear regular plastic canvas;
stitch 1

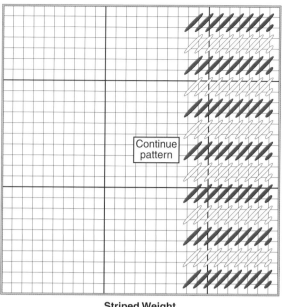

**Striped Weight**
27 holes x 27 holes
Cut 2 from clear regular plastic canvas;
stitch 1

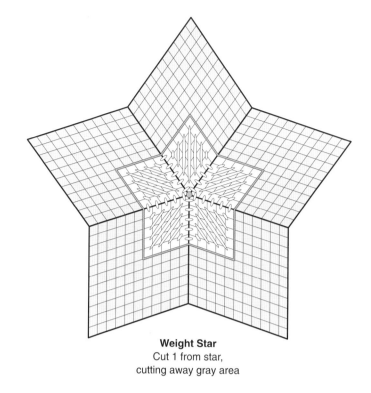

**Weight Star**
Cut 1 from star,
cutting away gray area

# Uncle Sam Teddy Bear

Design by Angie Arickx

**Size:** 10⅛ inches W x 9⅝ inches H
(25.7cm x 24.4cm)
**Skill Level:** Beginner

## Materials

❑ 1 sheet clear 7-count plastic canvas
❑ Uniek Needloft plastic canvas yarn as listed in color key
❑ #16 tapestry needle
❑ Sawtooth hanger
❑ Hot-glue gun

### Stitching Step-by-Step

**1** Cut plastic canvas according to graph.

**2** Stitch plastic canvas according to graph, filling in uncoded areas with dark royal Continental Stitches.

**3** When background stitching is complete, Backstitch mouth using brown yarn.

**4** Overcast edges according to graph.

**5** Hot-glue or stitch sawtooth hanger to back of teddy bear at center top.

**COLOR KEY**

| Yards | | Plastic Canvas Yarn |
|---|---|---|
| 8 (7.3m) | ■ | Burgundy #03 |
| 1 (0.9m) | ▨ | Cinnamon #14 |
| 2 (1.8m) | ▨ | Brown #15 |
| 14 (12.8m) | □ | Eggshell #39 |
| 12 (11m) | ▨ | Camel #43 |
| 9 (8.2m) | | Uncoded areas are dark royal #48 Continental Stitches |
| | ⁄ | Dark royal #48 Overcasting |
| | ⁄ | Brown #15 Backstitch |

Color numbers given are for Uniek Needloft plastic canvas yarn.

**Teddy Bear**
67 holes x 64 holes
Cut 1

# Let Freedom Ring

Design by Robin Howard-Will

**Size:** 10¼ inches W x 29 inches H, including hanger
(26cm x 73.4cm)

**Skill Level:** Beginner

## Materials

- ❏ 2 sheets clear 7-count plastic canvas
- ❏ Uniek Needloft plastic canvas yarn as listed in color key
- ❏ ¼-inch-wide (0.6cm) picot-edge satin ribbon:
  - 1 yard (0.9m) red
  - 1 yard (0.9m) blue
- ❏ 5 yards (4.6m) ⅛-inch (0.3cm) jute twine
- ❏ 8 (1½-inch/3.8cm) gold liberty bells
- ❏ Polyester fiberfill
- ❏ Hot-glue gun

## Stitching Step-by-Step

### Cutting & Stitching

**1** Cut two banners and 12 stars from plastic canvas according to graphs.

**2** Stitch banner pieces according to graphs, filling in uncoded areas with white Continental Stitches.

**3** Stitch uncoded stars, filling six with red Continental Stitches and six with royal Continental Stitches.

### Assembly & Finishing

**1** From jute twine, cut one 40-inch (1m) piece, three 30-inch (76cm) pieces, and two 20-inch (50.8cm) pieces.

**2** Fold one 30-inch (76cm) piece of jute in half; knot each end and tie a loop knot in center. Set aside for hanger.

**3** Onto each of the remaining jute strands, thread one bell; push bell to center of strand, and fold strand in half at bell; knot above bell. Knot cut ends of strand together at opposite end.

**4** Referring to Chimes Assembly Diagram, sandwich jute of bell chimes made from 20- and 30-inch strands between pairs of matching stars, wrong sides facing; using white yarn, Whipstitch stars together.

**5** Whipstitch two pairs of stars to jute on longest bell chime, knotting jute below the upper star as shown.

**6** Sandwich ends of bell chimes between bottom edges of stitched banner pieces where indicated by green dots on graph. Sandwich ends of hanger between top edges of banner for hanger where indicated by green dots. Using white yarn, Whipstitch banner pieces together, holding bell chimes and hanger in position, and stuffing banner with fiberfill before closing.

**7** Cut each piece of picot-edge ribbon into three 12-inch (30.5cm) pieces.

**8** Hold one piece of both colors of ribbon together, ends even. Thread ribbons through one of the remaining bells; tie ribbons in a bow. Repeat with remaining bells and ribbons.

**9** Hot-glue ribbon bows to banner as shown in photo.

**Hanger**

**Banner**

**COLOR KEY**

| Yards | Plastic Canvas Yarn |
|-------|---------------------|
| 12 (11m) | ■ Black #00 |
| 15 (13.7m) | ■ Red #01 |
| 14 (12.8m) | ▨ Royal #32 |
| 30 (27.4m) | Uncoded areas on banner are white #41 Continental Stitches |
| | 6 uncoded stars are red #01 Continental Stitches |
| | 6 uncoded stars are royal #32 Continental Stitches |
| ⟋ | White Overcasting |
| ● | Attach jute knot |

Color numbers given are for Uniek Needloft plastic canvas yarn.

**20" Strand**  **30" Strand**  **30" Strand**  **20" Strand**

**Bell**  **40" Strand**  **Tie Knot**

**Chimes Assembly Diagram**

**Star**
17 holes x 17 holes
Cut 12

**Banner**
67 holes x 49 holes
Cut 2

# Halloween Howler Holiday Holder

Design by Debbie Tabor

**Size:** 8½ inches W x 9¾ inches H x 5½ inches D
(21.6cm x 24.8cm x 14cm)

**Skill Level:** Intermediate

## Materials

- ❑ 2½ sheets clear 7-count plastic canvas
- ❑ Uniek Needloft plastic canvas yarn as listed in color key
- ❑ 6-strand cotton embroidery floss as listed in color key
- ❑ #16 tapestry needle
- ❑ Hot-glue gun

## Stitching Step-by-Step

### Cutting & Stitching

**1** Cut one cat body, two paws, one leaf, one basket base and one basket from plastic canvas according to graphs. Carefully trim gray portions out of basket base and leaf according to graphs.

**2** Stitch body, paws, leaf, basket base and basket with yarn according to graphs, reversing one paw before stitching and filling in uncoded areas on body and paws with black Continental Stitches. Leave uncoded area of basket base unstitched. Leave pink lines on body unstitched; basket and paws will be Whipstitched to howler along these lines during assembly.

**3** When background stitching is complete, using 6 strands embroidery floss, work embroidery: *lime green*—Backstitch around bottom of cat's eyes; *white*—work French Knot eye highlights, wrapping floss twice around needle, and all other Backstitch and Straight Stitch on black cat; *black*—Backstitch on jack-o'-lantern basket.

**4** Overcast top edge of basket between blue dots using yellow.

### Assembly

**1** Shape basket by gently bending in bottoms of basket so that green dots meet; using bittersweet yarn, Whipstitch curved edges together.

**2** For each bend in leaf, hold edges right sides together and using Christmas green yarn, tightly Whipstitch each cutout area of leaf and basket base pieces together according to the Dart Illustration.

**3** Using black for ears and matching colors elsewhere, Overcast edges of howler body, paws, leaf and basket base, leaving body and paws unstitched between arrows.

**4** Using black yarn, Whipstitch tops of paws between arrows to shoulders of howler body between arrows; using bright orange, Whipstitch basket side edges to howler body where indicated by pink lines on body graph. Using Christmas green yarn, Whipstitch basket base to bottom of basket and to bottom edge of body between arrows; tack one end of leaf to center bottom of basket base.

**5** Overcast all remaining edges of howler basket using adjacent colors.

**6** Using black yarn, stitch paws to basket sides.

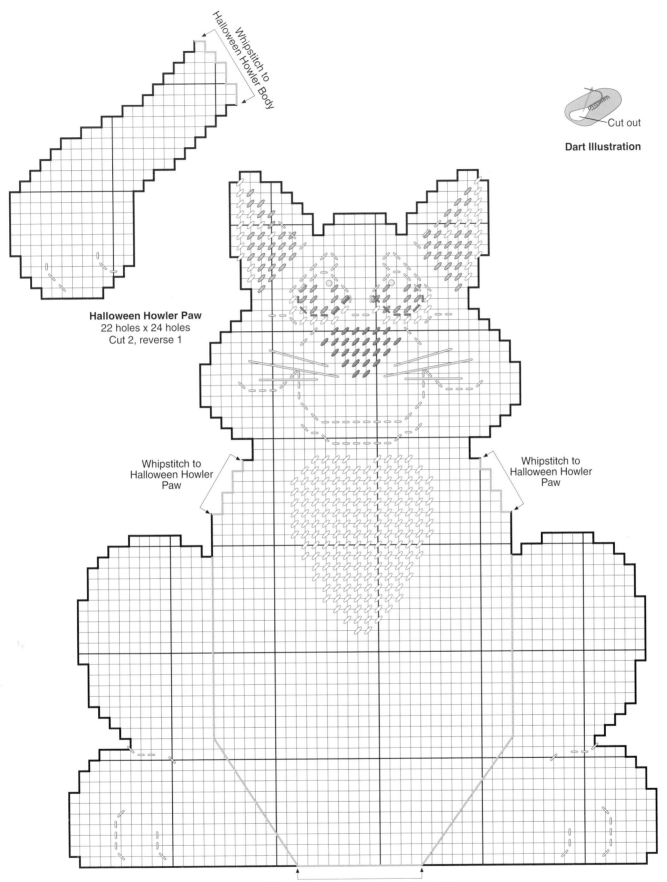

**Dart Illustration**

Cut out

**Halloween Howler Paw**
22 holes x 24 holes
Cut 2, reverse 1

Whipstitch to Halloween Howler Body

Whipstitch to
Halloween Howler
Paw

Whipstitch to
Halloween Howler
Paw

Whipstitch to Halloween Howler Basket Base

**Halloween Howler Body**
57 holes x 65 holes
Cut 1

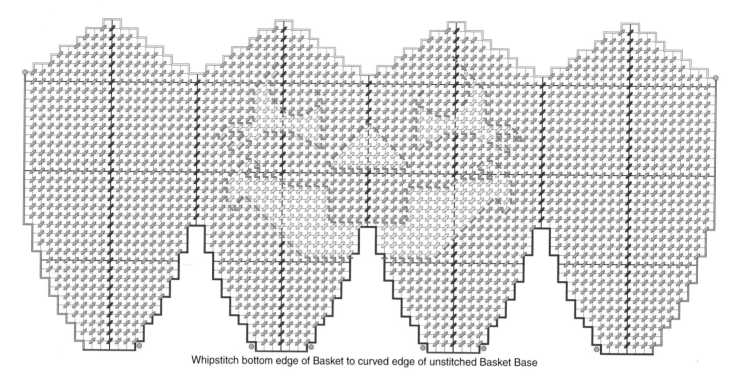

Whipstitch bottom edge of Basket to curved edge of unstitched Basket Base

**Halloween Howler Basket**
80 holes x 37 holes
Cut 1

**COLOR KEY**

| Yards | Plastic Canvas Yarn |
|---|---|
| 2 (1.8m) | ☐ Pink #07 |
| 11 (10m) | ☐ Christmas green #28 |
| 8 (7.3m) | ☐ White #41 |
| 9 (8.2m) | ■ Bittersweet #52 |
| 1 (0.9m) | ☐ Watermelon #55 |
| 7 (6.4m) | ☐ Yellow #57 |
| 31 (28.4m) | ☐ Bright orange #58 |
| 36 (32.9m) | Uncoded areas on cat and paw are black #00 Continental Stitches |
| | ⁄ Black #00 Overcasting and Whipstitching |

**6-Strand Embroidery Floss**

| | |
|---|---|
| 6 (5.5m) | ⁄ Black Backstitch |
| 4 (3.7m) | ⁄ White Backstitch and Straight Stitch |
| 1 (0.9m) | ⁄ Lime Backstitch |
| | ○ White French Knot (2 wraps) |

Color numbers given are for Uniek Needloft plastic canvas yarn.

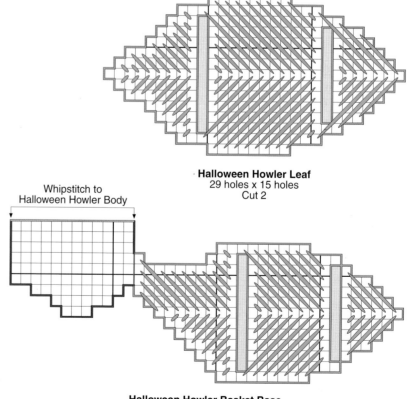

**Halloween Howler Leaf**
29 holes x 15 holes
Cut 2

Whipstitch to
Halloween Howler Body

**Halloween Howler Basket Base**
38 holes x 15 holes
Cut 1

# Halloween Shelf Sitters

Designs by Joan Green

## Size:

**Black cat:** 7 inches W x 7⅛ inches H
(17.8cm x 18.1cm)

**Ghost:** 6 inches W x 7 inches H
(15.2cm x 17.8cm)

**Jack-o'-lantern:** 5⅞ inches W x 6⅛ inches H
(14.9cm x 15.6cm)

**Skill Level:** Beginner

## Materials

❑ 1½ sheets clear 7-count plastic canvas
❑ Worsted weight yarn as listed in color key
❑ #16 tapestry needle

## Stitching Step-by-Step

**1** Cut center, right side and back side pieces for each character from plastic canvas according to graphs.

**2** Stitch plastic canvas according to graphs.

**3** *When background stitching is complete, work embroidery stitches:* Using black throughout, work French Knot eyes on cat; Backstitch mouth and eyes on ghost. Using bright yellow throughout, stitch noses on cat and ghost, working bottom layer of Slanted Gobelin Stitches in one direction, then top layer in the other; Backstitch mouth on cat.

**4** Using adjacent colors throughout, Whipstitch pieces of each character together along seams, keeping bottom edges even and stitching through each pair of holes twice. Overcast remaining edges.

**5** Bend characters along seams accordion-style to make them stand.

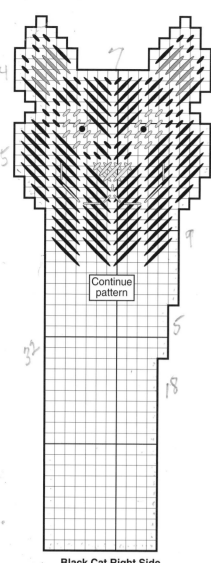

**Black Cat Right Side**
19 holes x 50 holes
Cut 1

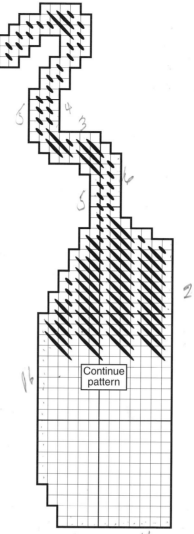

**Black Cat Left Side**
17 holes x 49 holes
Cut 1

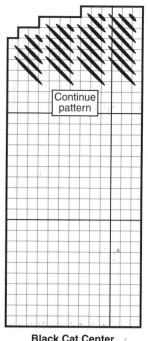

**Black Cat Center**
13 holes x 30 holes
Cut 1

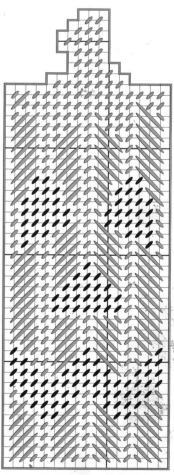

**Jack-o'-Lantern Center**
16 holes x 43 holes
Cut 1

**COLOR KEY**

| Yards | Worsted Weight Yarn |
|---|---|
| 30 (27.4m) | ■ Black |
| 26 (23.8m) | ▨ Orange |
| 22 (20.1m) | □ White |
| 2 (1.8m) | ▦ Blue-green |
| 1 (0.9m) | ▨ Bright yellow |
| 1 (0.9m) | ▨ Apple green |
| | ╱ Black Backstitch |
| | ╱ Bright yellow Backstitch |
| | ● Black French Knot |

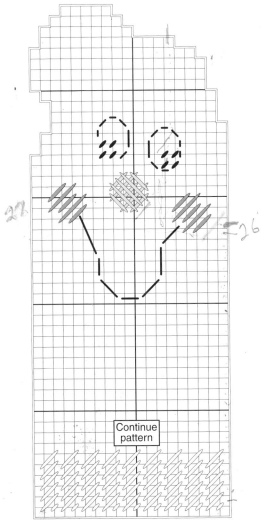

**Ghost Center**
19 holes x 48 holes
Cut 1

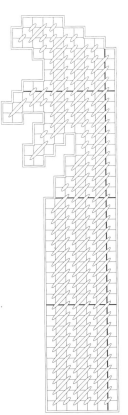

**Ghost Left Side**
11 holes x 37 holes
Cut 1

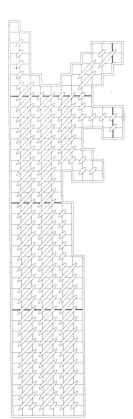

**Ghost Right Side**
11 holes x 37 holes
Cut 1

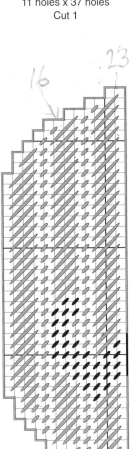

**Jack-o'-Lantern Left Side**
12 holes x 35 holes
Cut 1

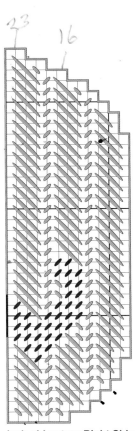

**Jack-o'-Lantern Right Side**
12 holes x 35 holes
Cut 1

# Skeleton

Design by Phyllis Dobbs

**Size:** 10¼ inches W x 23 inches L (26cm x 58.4cm)
**Skill Level:** Beginner

## Materials

❑ 1 artist-size sheet of clear 7-count plastic canvas
❑ Uniek Needloft plastic canvas yarn as listed in color key
❑ #16 tapestry needle
❑ Sawtooth hanger
❑ Hot-glue gun

### Stitching Step-by-Step

**1** Cut one skeleton, one pumpkin and one hat according to graphs.

**2** Stitch skeleton, pumpkin and hat according to graphs. Using adjacent colors, Overcast edges of pumpkin and hat. Using black, Overcast skeleton.

**3** Cut one 5-inch (12.7cm) piece of fern yarn. Referring to photo throughout, hot-glue ends of yarn to wrong side of stitched pumpkin. Hot-glue yarn pumpkin hanger to wrong side of skeleton's hand.

**4** Hot-glue hat to skeleton as shown.

**5** Stitch or hot-glue sawtooth hanger to wrong side of skeleton.

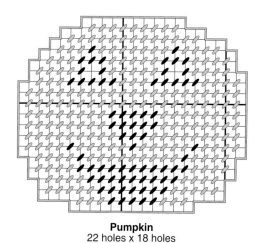

**Pumpkin**
22 holes x 18 holes
Cut 1

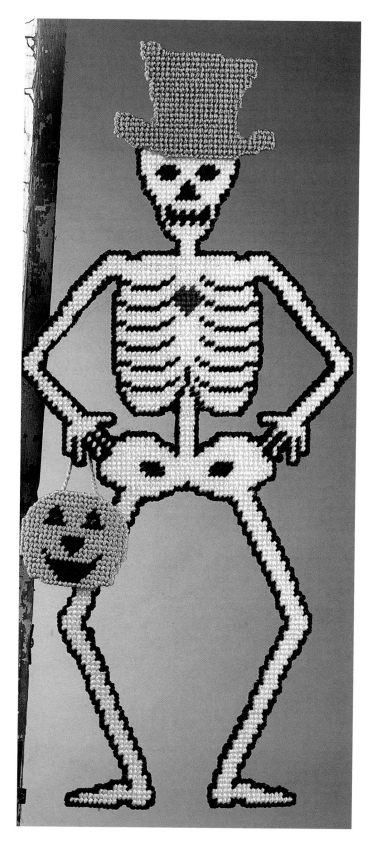

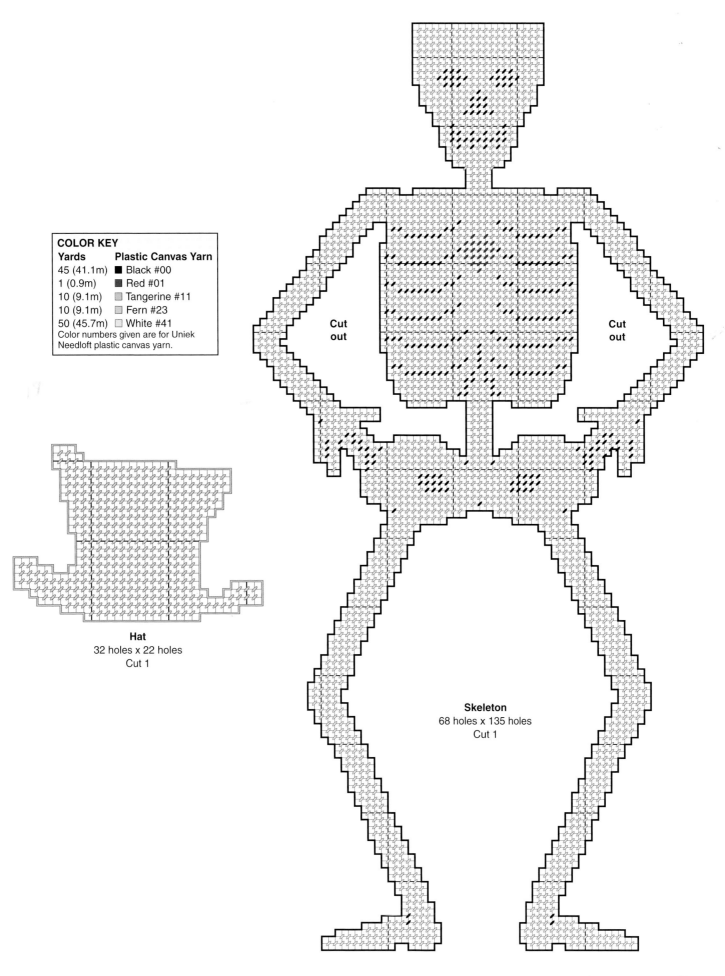

**COLOR KEY**

| Yards | Plastic Canvas Yarn |
|---|---|
| 45 (41.1m) | ■ Black #00 |
| 1 (0.9m) | ■ Red #01 |
| 10 (9.1m) | ▨ Tangerine #11 |
| 10 (9.1m) | ▨ Fern #23 |
| 50 (45.7m) | ☐ White #41 |

Color numbers given are for Uniek Needloft plastic canvas yarn.

**Hat**
32 holes x 22 holes
Cut 1

**Skeleton**
68 holes x 135 holes
Cut 1

Cut out

Cut out

# Batty Belfry

Design by Janelle Giese

**Size:** 7 inches W x 13 inches H (17.8cm x 33cm), excluding hanger

**Skill Level:** Beginner

## Materials

- ❏ 1 sheet clear 7-count plastic canvas
- ❏ Uniek Needloft plastic canvas yarn as listed in color key
- ❏ Kreinik Heavy (#32) Glow-in-the-Dark Braid as listed in color key
- ❏ DMC #3 pearl cotton as listed in color key
- ❏ #16 tapestry needle
- ❏ 3 (½-inch/13mm) silver liberty bells
- ❏ 12 (7mm) silver jump rings
- ❏ 2mm silver chain:
  - 1 (8-inch/20.3cm) piece
  - 3 (1-inch/2.5cm) pieces
  - 2 (½-inch/1.3cm) pieces
- ❏ Needle-nose or jewelry pliers
- ❏ Hot-glue gun

## Stitching Step-by-Step

### Cutting & Stitching

**1** Cut vampire and bat from plastic canvas according to graphs.

**2** Stitch vampire and bat according to graphs.

**3** Using adjacent colors, Overcast edges.

**4** Using 1 ply separated from a length of watermelon yarn, stitch vampire's cheeks and nose, and flower on lapel. Work yellow 1-wrap French Knot in center of flower on lapel.

**5** Using lemon-lime heavy (#32) glow-in-the-dark braid, Backstitch eyes, Straight Stitch fangs, and work reverse Continental Stitches over stitches of pumpkin according to graph.

**6** Using black #3 pearl cotton, work all remaining Backstitches and Straight Stitches; work French Knot buttons on vampire's shirt, wrapping cotton around needle once. Using bright orange yarn, work French Knot center in flower on lapel, wrapping yarn around needle once.

### Assembly

**1** Attach a jump ring to vampire and bat at each position indicated by a red dot on graphs.

**2** Attach one end of the 8-inch (20.3cm) piece of chain to each jump ring at top of vampire for hanger. Suspend bat from bottom of vampire with two 1-inch (2.5cm) pieces of chain.

**3** Attach a bell to one end of each ½-inch (1.2cm) piece of chain and to remaining 1-inch (2.5cm) piece of chain; attach other ends of chains to jump rings in bottom of bat.

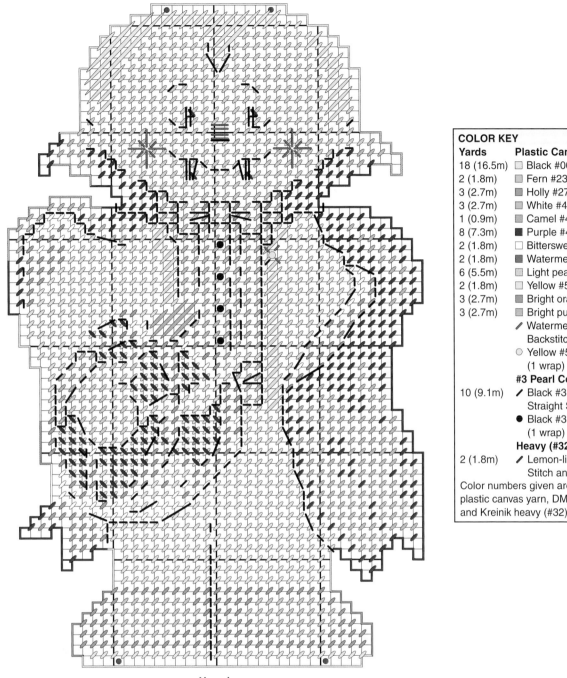

**Vampire**
40 holes x 62 holes
Cut 1

**COLOR KEY**

| Yards | Plastic Canvas Yarn |
|---|---|
| 18 (16.5m) | Black #00 |
| 2 (1.8m) | Fern #23 |
| 3 (2.7m) | Holly #27 |
| 3 (2.7m) | White #41 |
| 1 (0.9m) | Camel #43 |
| 8 (7.3m) | Purple #46 |
| 2 (1.8m) | Bittersweet #52 |
| 2 (1.8m) | Watermelon #55 |
| 6 (5.5m) | Light peach #56 |
| 2 (1.8m) | Yellow #57 |
| 3 (2.7m) | Bright orange #58 |
| 3 (2.7m) | Bright purple #64 |
| | ✎ Watermelon #55 1-ply Backstitch and Straight Stitch |
| | ○ Yellow #57 French Knot (1 wrap) |

**#3 Pearl Cotton**

| | |
|---|---|
| 10 (9.1m) | ✎ Black #310 Backstitch and Straight Stitch |
| | ● Black #310 French Knot (1 wrap) |

**Heavy (#32) Glow-in-the-Dark Braid**

| | |
|---|---|
| 2 (1.8m) | ✎ Lemon-lime #054F Straight Stitch and Reverse Continental Stitch |

Color numbers given are for Uniek Needloft plastic canvas yarn, DMC #3 pearl cotton and Kreinik heavy (#32) braid.

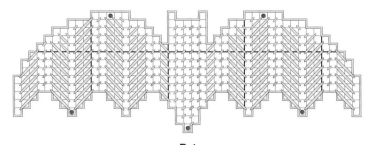

**Bat**
45 holes x 15
Cut 1

# Best Witches

Design by Vicki Blizzard

**Size:** 14 inches W x 9½ inches H
(35.6cm x 24.1cm)
**Skill Level:** Intermediate

## Materials

❏ Uniek QuickCount 7-count plastic canvas:
  1½ sheets clear
  ¼ sheet black
❏ Worsted weight yarn as listed in color key
❏ DMC #3 pearl cotton as listed in color key
❏ 6-strand cotton embroidery floss as listed in color key
❏ Round black cabochons from The Beadery:
  3 (4mm)
  6 (6mm)
❏ Satin ribbon:
  6 inches (15.2cm) ⅛-inch-wide (0.3cm) purple
  6 inches (15.2cm) ⅛-inch-wide (0.3cm) black
  2 yards (1.8m) ⅛-inch-wide (0.3cm) green
  24 inches (61cm) ¼-inch-wide (0.6cm) orange

❏ Orange felt
❏ #16 tapestry needle
❏ Hot-glue gun

## Stitching Step-by-Step

### Cutting

**1** Cut three pumpkins, three bodies, three faces, three muzzles, six ears, six arms, one of each sign, two hats A and one hat B from clear plastic canvas according to graphs.

**2** Cut two pumpkin eyes, one pumpkin mouth, one cat and one spider from black plastic canvas according to graphs.

### Stitching

**1** Stitch pumpkins, pumpkin eyes and mouth, spider, cat and signs according to graphs; Overcast according to graphs.

**2** When background stitching is complete, using black #3 pearl cotton, Backstitch signs according to graphs. Using black yarn, work French Knots at bottom of cat according to graph.

**3** *Using white embroidery floss, work spiderweb on one pumpkin only:* Referring to photo throughout, stitch five long "spokes" first. Bring white floss up at red dot nearest center of spiderweb; carry floss across web, wrapping it around each spoke, and take it down at red heart nearest center of web. Repeat to add webbing in remaining two positions according to graph.

**4** Stitch one hat A and hat B according to graphs. Reverse remaining hat A and stitch, substituting purple for dark gray.

**5** Stitch bodies according to graph, substituting purple on one body and dark gray on another.

**6** Stitch two arms according to graph, reversing one before stitching. Stitch two arms substituting purple for bright green, reversing one arm before stitching. Stitch remaining arms substituting dark gray for bright green, reversing one arm before stitching.

**7** Stitch faces, muzzles and ears; Overcast according to graphs. Using very dark mahogany #3 pearl cotton, Backstitch muzzles according to graphs.

## Assembly

**1** Referring to photo throughout, center and hot-glue face to top front of each body. Hot-glue muzzle to each face. Hot-glue hat matching body color to top front of each head. Hot-glue ears to sides of head directly below hat.

**2** Center and hot-glue assembled bear to top edge of each pumpkin, gluing dark gray bear to pumpkin with spiderweb. Hot-glue matching arms to body and pumpkin so that hands touch in center. Center and hot-glue 4mm cabochon to top of each muzzle for nose. Hot-glue two 6mm cabochons to each face between hat and muzzle for eyes.

**3** Cut orange ribbon into three 8-inch (20.3cm) pieces. Tie each in a bow; trim ends. Center and hot-glue bow to top of each body under chin. Cut a 12-inch (30.5cm) piece of green ribbon; tie in a bow around cat's neck.

**4** Cut a 6-inch (15.2cm) piece of green ribbon; tie in a small bow and trim ends. Hot-glue to right side of purple hat. Tie black and purple ribbons in small bows; trim ends. Center and hot-glue black ribbon to top of bright green hat; hot-glue purple ribbon to left side of dark gray hat.

**5** Cut three 8-inch (20.3cm) pieces green ribbon. Tie a knot in one end of one piece; thread this piece from back to front through hole in upper left-hand corner of one sign, then from front to back through hole in upper right-hand corner of sign. Adjust ribbon to leave a 4-inch (10.2cm) hanging loop; knot end on back and trim. Repeat with remaining signs.

**6** Position pumpkin with purple bear on left, pumpkin with spiderweb and dark gray bear on right, and pumpkin with bright green bear in center as shown. Hot-glue pumpkins together where they overlap, positioning center pumpkin slightly lower.

**7** Hot-glue cat to lower left front of left pumpkin. Center and hot-glue spider to bottom of spiderweb. Hot-glue eyes and mouth to center pumpkin.

**8** Hang signs over bears' hands so that they read "BEARY BEST WITCHES FOR A HAPPY HALLOWEEN."

**9** *Hanger:* Thread remaining green ribbon through outer corners at top of left- and right-hand pumpkins. Adjust ribbon, leaving hanging loop of desired size; knot ribbon ends on back.

**Muzzle**
7 holes x 4 holes
Cut 3 from clear plastic canvas

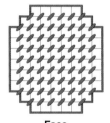

**Face**
9 holes x 10 holes
Cut 3 from clear plastic canvas

| COLOR KEY | |
|---|---|
| **Yards** | **Worsted Weight Yarn** |
| 36 (32.9m) | Orange |
| 9 (8.2m) | Bright green |
| 8 (7.3m) | Dark gray |
| 8 (7.3m) | Dark brown |
| 8 (7.3m) | Black |
| 3 (2.7m) | Almond |
| 9 (8.2m) | Uncoded areas on signs are white Continental Stitches |
| 8 (7.3m) | ✏ Purple Overcasting |
| | ● Black French Knot |
| | **#3 Pearl Cotton** |
| 1 (0.9m) | ✏ Very dark mahogany #300 Backstitch |
| 3 (2.7m) | ✏ Black #310 Backstitch |
| | **6-Strand Embroidery Floss** |
| 1 (0.9m) | ✏ White Straight Stitch |

Color numbers given are for DMC #3 pearl cotton.

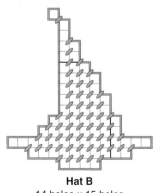

**Hat B**
14 holes x 15 holes
Cut 1 from clear plastic canvas

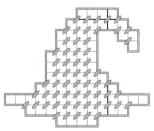

**Hat A**
14 holes x 11 holes
Cut 2 from clear plastic canvas;
Stitch 1 as shown;
Reverse 1 and stitch,
substituting purple for dark gray

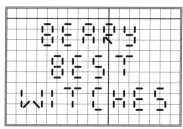

**Sign A**
17 holes x 11 holes
Cut 1 from clear plastic canvas

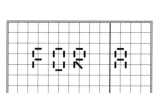

**Sign B**
14 holes x 7 holes
Cut 1 from clear plastic canvas

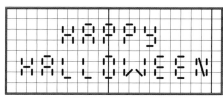

**Sign C**
21 holes x 8 holes
Cut 1 from clear plastic canvas

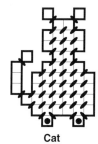

**Cat**
8 holes x 11 holes
Cut 1 from black plastic canvas

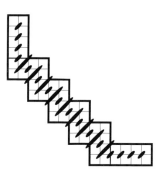

**Pumpkin Mouth**
14 holes x 14 holes
Cut 1 from black plastic canvas

**Pumpkin Eye**
6 holes x 6 holes
Cut 2 from black plastic canvas

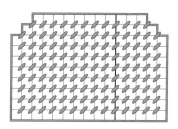

**Body**
15 holes x 10 holes
Cut 3 from clear plastic canvas;
Stitch 1 as shown;
Stitch 1 substituting purple for bright green;
Stitch 1 substituting dark gray for bright green

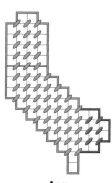

**Arm**
10 holes x 15 holes
Cut 6 from clear plastic canvas
Stitch 2, reversing 1, as graphed
Stitch 2, reversing 1,
substituting purple for bright green
Stitch 2, reversing 1,
substituting dark gray for bright green

**Spider**
8 holes x 5 holes
Cut 1 from black plastic canvas
Cut away blue lines,
leaving black lines only

**Ear**
3 holes x 3 holes
Cut 6 from clear plastic canvas

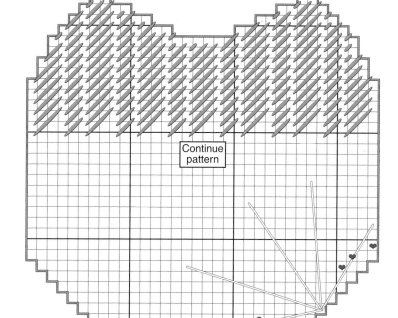

**Pumpkin**
34 holes x 33 holes
Cut 3 from clear plastic canvas
Stitch spiderweb on 1 only

**COLOR KEY**

| Yards | Worsted Weight Yarn |
|---|---|
| 36 (32.9m) | Orange |
| 9 (8.2m) | Bright green |
| 8 (7.3m) | Dark gray |
| 8 (7.3m) | Dark brown |
| 8 (7.3m) | Black |
| 3 (2.7m) | Almond |
| 9 (8.2m) | Uncoded areas on signs are white Continental Stitches |
| 8 (7.3m) | ╱ Purple Overcasting |
| | ● Black French Knot |
| **#3 Pearl Cotton** | |
| 1 (0.9m) | ╱ Very dark mahogany #300 Backstitch |
| 3 (2.7m) | ╱ Black #310 Backstitch |
| **6-Strand Embroidery Floss** | |
| 1 (0.9m) | ╱ White Straight Stitch |

Color numbers given are for DMC #3 pearl cotton.

# Autumn Silhouettes

Design by Ronda Bryce

***Size:*** Fits boutique-style tissue box
***Skill Level:*** Beginner

## Materials

- ❏ 2 sheets Uniek QuickCount black 7-count plastic canvas
- ❏ Coats & Clark Red Heart Super Saver worsted weight yarn Art. E301 as listed in color key
- ❏ Black thread
- ❏ 3 (9 x 12-inch/22.9cm x 30.5cm) sheets dark orange felt
- ❏ #16 tapestry needle
- ❏ Sewing needle
- ❏ Craft knife or plastic canvas cutter

### Stitching Step-by-Step

**1** Cut sides and top from black plastic canvas according to graphs, carefully cutting out openings in each piece.

**2** Cut four pieces of dark orange felt 4⅝ x 5½ inches (11.8cm x 14cm) for sides, and one piece 4½ x 4½ inches (11.4cm x 11.4cm) for top.

**3** Using the plastic canvas top as a template, cut center opening in felt piece for top, cutting the opening slightly larger than opening in plastic canvas top.

**4** Using black yarn, stitch plastic canvas top and sides according to graphs, Overcasting edges of cutout openings.

**5** Using sewing needle and black thread, stitch corresponding pieces of felt to backs of stitched plastic canvas top and sides, trimming edges of felt as needed to allow room for Whipstitching plastic canvas pieces together.

**6** Using black yarn throughout, Whipstitch sides together; Whipstitch assembled sides to top. Overcast bottom edges.

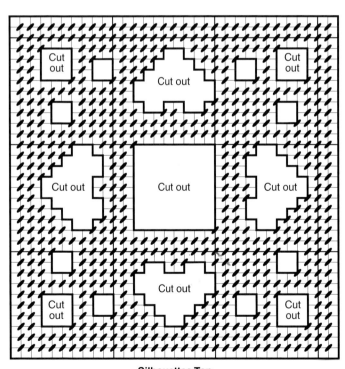

**Silhouettes Top**
32 holes x 32 holes
Cut 1

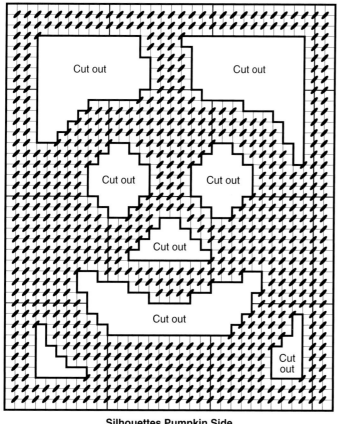

**Silhouettes Pumpkin Side**
32 holes x 38 holes
Cut 1

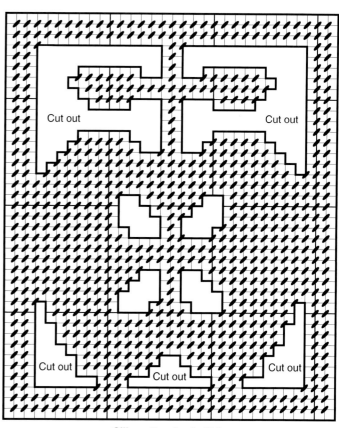

**Silhouettes Apple Side**
32 holes x 38 holes
Cut 1

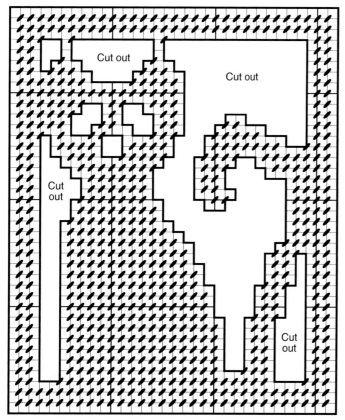

**Silhouettes Cat Side**
32 holes x 38 holes
Cut 1

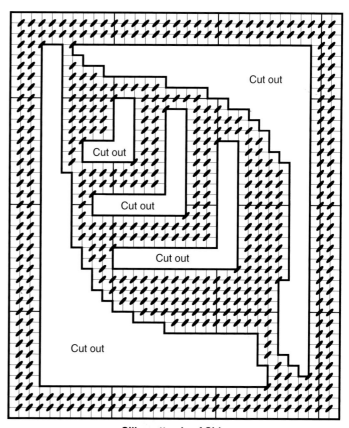

**Silhouettes Leaf Side**
32 holes x 38 holes
Cut 1

# Thankful Turkey Holiday Holder

Design by Debbie Tabor

**Size:** 9 inches W x 10 inches H x 6 inches D
(22.9cm x 25.4cm x 15.2cm)
**Skill Level:** Intermediate

## Materials

❑ 2½ sheets clear 7-count plastic canvas
❑ Uniek Needloft plastic canvas yarn as listed in color key
❑ 6-strand cotton embroidery floss as listed in color key
❑ #16 tapestry needle
❑ Blow-dry hair dryer
❑ Hot-glue gun

## Stitching Step-by-Step

### Cutting & Stitching

**1** Cut one turkey body, two turkey wings, one turkey basket base and one turkey basket from plastic canvas according to graphs.

**2** Stitch turkey, wings and basket with yarn according to graphs, reversing one wing before stitching and filling in uncoded areas on turkey and wings with camel Continental Stitches. Leave uncoded area of basket base unstitched. Leave pink lines on turkey body unstitched; basket and wings will be Whipstitched to turkey along these lines during assembly.

**3** When background stitching is complete, using 6 strands embroidery floss, work embroidery: *white*—French Knot highlights in turkey's eyes, wrapping floss twice around needle; *brown*—Backstitch corn; *light brown*—Backstitch fruit and vegetable stems on basket; *dark rust*—Backstitch pumpkin; *green*—Backstitch leaves; *black*—all other Backstitch and Straight Stitch on turkey.

**4** Overcast top edge of basket between blue dots using adjacent colors.

## Assembly

**1** Shape bottom of turkey by gently bending in bottom edge so that green dots meet; using camel yarn, Whipstitch curved edges together.

**2** In the same manner, shape basket by gently bending in bottoms of basket so that green dots meet; using adjacent colors, Whipstitch curved edges together.

**3** Using brown, Overcast edges of turkey and wings, leaving them unstitched at pink lines.

**4** Using camel yarn, Whipstitch along pink lines on wings to shoulders of turkey where indicated by pink lines; Whipstitch basket side edges to turkey where indicated by pink lines on turkey graph. Using yellow yarn, Whipstitch basket base to bottom of basket and to bottom edge of body between arrows.

**5** Overcast all remaining edges of turkey using adjacent colors.

**6** Using a blow-dry hair dryer set on LOW-heat setting, soften wing tips. Fold wings over edges of basket as shown. Using camel yarn, stitch folded wings to basket sides.

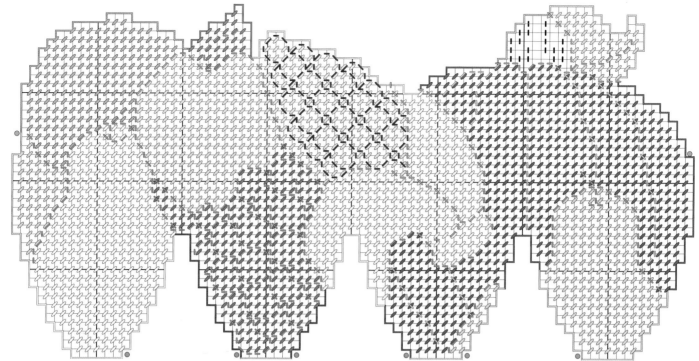

Whipstitch bottom edges of Basket to Basket Base where indicated by pink lines on base

**Thankful Turkey Basket**
80 holes x 40 holes
Cut 1

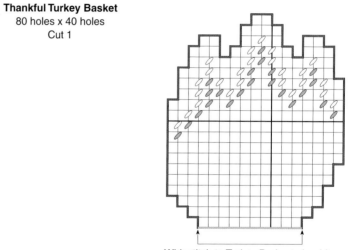

Whipstitch to Turkey Body at shoulder

**Thankful Turkey Wing**
17 holes x 20 holes

**COLOR KEY**

| Yards | Plastic Canvas Yarn |
|---|---|
| 1 (0.9m) | ■ Black #00 |
| 6 (5.5m) | □ Christmas red #02 |
| 6 (5.5m) | ■ Rust #09 |
| 9 (8.2m) | □ Tangerine #11 |
| 3 (2.7m) | □ Lemon #20 |
| 2 (1.8m) | ■ Christmas green #28 |
| 1 (0.9m) | □ White #41 |
| 5 (4.6m) | ■ Purple #46 |
| 10 (9.1m) | ■ Bittersweet #52 |
| 2 (1.8m) | □ Mermaid #53 |
| 9 (8.2m) | □ Turquoise #54 |
| 4 (3.7m) | □ Yellow #57 |
| 10 (9.1m) | ■ Bright orange #58 |
| 8 (7.3m) | □ Bright green #61 |
| 62 (56.7m) | Uncoded areas on turkey and wing are camel #43 Continental Stitches |
| 6 (5.5m) | ✐ Brown #15 Overcasting and Whipstitch |
| | ✐ Camel #43 Overcasting |

**6-Strand Embroidery Floss**

| | |
|---|---|
| 15 (13.7m) | ✐ Black Backstitch |
| 5 (4.6m) | ✐ Brown Backstitch |
| 3 (2.7m) | ✐ Light brown Backstitch |
| 2 (1.8m) | ✐ Green Backstitch |
| 1 (0.9m) | ✐ Dark rust Backstitch |
| 1 (0.9m) | ✐ White Backstitch |
| | ● White French Knot (2 wraps) |

Color numbers given are for Uniek Needloft plastic canvas yarn.

**Thankful Turkey Basket Base**
48 holes x 22 holes
Cut 1

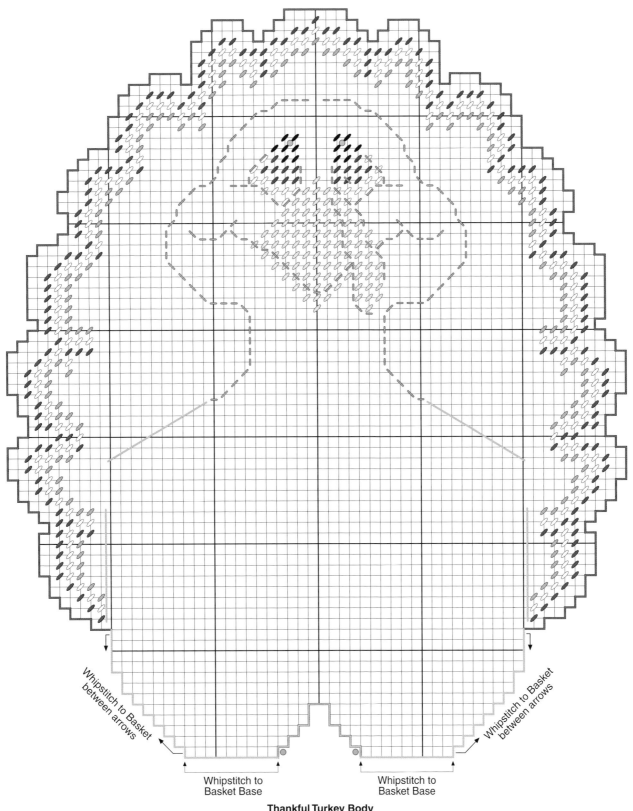

**Thankful Turkey Body**
60 holes x 70 holes
Cut 1

Whipstitch to Basket between arrows

Whipstitch to Basket between arrows

Whipstitch to
Basket Base

Whipstitch to
Basket Base

# Harvesttime Bread Basket

Design by Robin Howard-Will

**Size:** 9½ inches W x 9¼ inches H x 7¾ inches D
(24.1cm x 23.5cm x 19.7cm)

**Skill Level:** Beginner

## Materials

❑ 3 sheets clear 7-count plastic canvas
❑ Uniek Needloft plastic canvas yarn as listed in color key
❑ 4 (5mm) movable eyes
❑ #16 tapestry needle
❑ Hot-glue gun

## Stitching Step-by-Step

**1** Cut two bread basket sides, one handle, one bottom, two turkeys, two turkey tail feathers, four turkey wings and four turkey beaks from plastic canvas according to graphs.

**2** Stitch all pieces according to graphs, reversing two wings before stitching. Basket bottom will remain unstitched.

**3** Using maple yarn through step 4, Whipstitch short edges of basket sides together. Whipstitch bottom to assembled sides, positioning seams in center of long straight sides.

**4** Overcast long edges of handle. Center short ends of handle over seams; Whipstitch handle ends to top edge of basket and continue to Overcast top edge of basket.

**5** Using brown yarn, Overcast tail feathers and wings. Using yellow, Overcast turkey legs and feet; using brown, Overcast remaining edges of turkey.

**6** With wrong sides facing, Whipstitch two beaks together along straight edge using yellow yarn; Overcast remaining edges of beak. Repeat with remaining beak pieces.

**7** Referring to photo throughout, center and hot-glue one set of tail feathers over one of the seams in the basket. Center and hot-glue a turkey to the tail feathers. Hot-glue eyes to turkey where indicated on graph. Hot-glue Whipstitched edges of beak to turkey head above stitched cinnamon wattle. Hot-glue two wings to turkey. Repeat to hot-glue turkey to other side of basket.

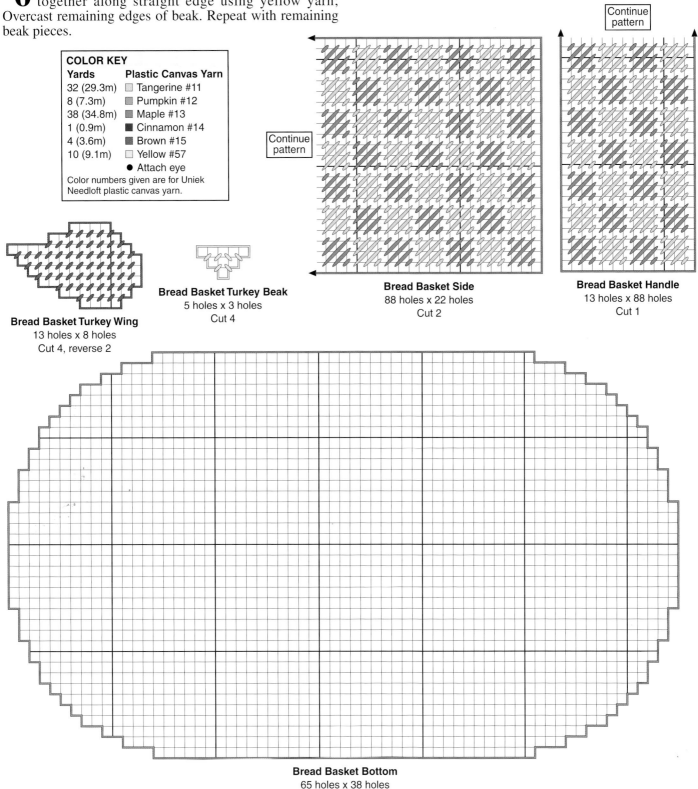

**COLOR KEY**

| Yards | Plastic Canvas Yarn |
|---|---|
| 32 (29.3m) | Tangerine #11 |
| 8 (7.3m) | Pumpkin #12 |
| 38 (34.8m) | Maple #13 |
| 1 (0.9m) | Cinnamon #14 |
| 4 (3.6m) | Brown #15 |
| 10 (9.1m) | Yellow #57 |
| ● | Attach eye |

Color numbers given are for Uniek Needloft plastic canvas yarn.

Continue pattern

Continue pattern

**Bread Basket Side**
88 holes x 22 holes
Cut 2

**Bread Basket Handle**
13 holes x 88 holes
Cut 1

**Bread Basket Turkey Wing**
13 holes x 8 holes
Cut 4, reverse 2

**Bread Basket Turkey Beak**
5 holes x 3 holes
Cut 4

**Bread Basket Bottom**
65 holes x 38 holes
Cut 1

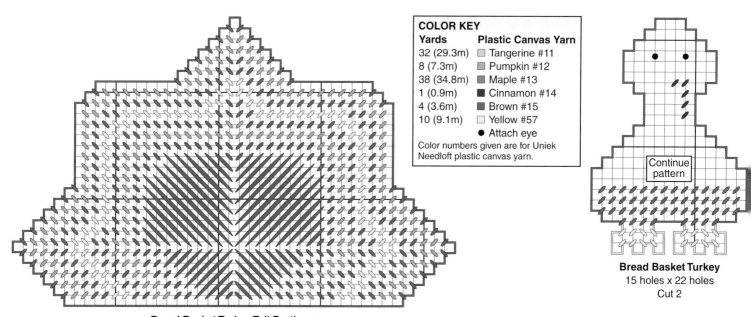

**COLOR KEY**

| Yards | Plastic Canvas Yarn |
|---|---|
| 32 (29.3m) | ☐ Tangerine #11 |
| 8 (7.3m) | ☐ Pumpkin #12 |
| 38 (34.8m) | ☐ Maple #13 |
| 1 (0.9m) | ☐ Cinnamon #14 |
| 4 (3.6m) | ☐ Brown #15 |
| 10 (9.1m) | ☐ Yellow #57 |
| ● Attach eye | |

Color numbers given are for Uniek Needloft plastic canvas yarn.

**Bread Basket Turkey Tail Feathers**
43 holes x 27 holes
Cut 2

Continue pattern

**Bread Basket Turkey**
15 holes x 22 holes
Cut 2

# Bluebird Coaster Set

Designs by Vicki Blizzard

**Size:** 4½ inches W x 7 inches H x 2 inches D
(11.4cm x 17.8cm x 5.1cm)
**Skill Level:** Intermediate

## Materials

❑ 2 sheets clear 7-count plastic canvas
❑ Worsted weight yarn as listed in color key
❑ #16 tapestry needle
❑ 8 (8mm) round black cabochons
❑ Hot-glue gun

### Stitching Step-by-Step

#### Coasters

**1** Cut four bluebird coasters, four small holly leaves and four hats from plastic canvas according to graphs.

**2** Stitch plastic canvas according to graphs. Using royal blue and bright yellow, Overcast bluebirds; using bright green and white, Overcast hats; Using bright green, Overcast small holly leaves.

**3** When background stitching is complete, using yellow, Straight Stitch beaks; using bright green, Straight Stitch centers of holly leaves; and work scarlet French Knot at one end of each leaf.

**4** Cut four 6-inch (15.2cm) lengths and four 36-inch (0.9m) lengths white yarn. Wrap one longer piece around index finger of one hand. Slide loops off finger and wrap shorter length around center; knot tightly. Clip loops and fray ends; trim to form ¾-inch (1.9cm) pompom. Tie pompom where indicated on hat graph; trim yarn ends to 6 inches (15.2cm). Repeat with remaining yarn to make three more pompoms.

**5** Hot-glue small holly leaves to hats and cabochons to birds according to graph. Referring to photo, hot-glue hats to heads.

**6** Cut eight 12-inch (30.5cm) lengths of bright green yarn. Hold two lengths together; tie in a bow around one bird's neck. Repeat for remaining bluebirds.

## Coaster Holder

**1** Cut gingerbread house coaster holder front, back, sides, roof trim, perches, heart, eight large holly leaves, fence, five poinsettias and three snowflakes from plastic canvas according to graphs. Cut also one piece 31 holes by 13 holes for coaster holder bottom; it will remain unstitched.

**2** Stitch coaster holder front, back, sides, heart, holly leaves and perches according to graphs, reversing one side before stitching.

**3** When background stitching is complete, using bright green, Straight Stitch centers of holly leaves and Overcast edges. Using scarlet throughout, Overcast heart and roof trim; Whipstitch perches together, wrong sides facing.

**4** Using camel throughout, Overcast edges of front opening. Whipstitch sides to front between dots, then Whipstitch back to sides, keeping all bottom edges

even. Whipstitch unstitched bottom to assembled coaster holder. Overcast remaining edges of coaster holder.

**5** Stitch and Overcast fence and snowflakes according to graphs; Straight Stitch fence.

**6** Using scarlet, Overcast poinsettias; using 2 plies separated from a length of bright yellow, work French Knots in centers.

**7** Referring to photo throughout, hot-glue roof trim, heart and fence to coaster holder. Hot-glue snowflakes to roof trim and poinsettias to fence.

**8** Hot-glue holly leaves around opening, overlapping them slightly. Center and hot-glue base of perch under wreath. Cut three 12-inch lengths of scarlet yarn; holding them together, tie them in a bow. Hot-glue bow to bottom of wreath.

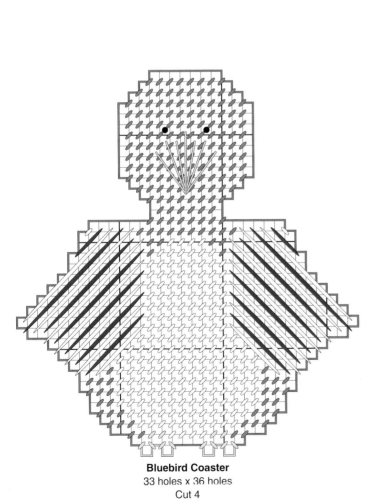

**Bluebird Coaster**
33 holes x 36 holes
Cut 4

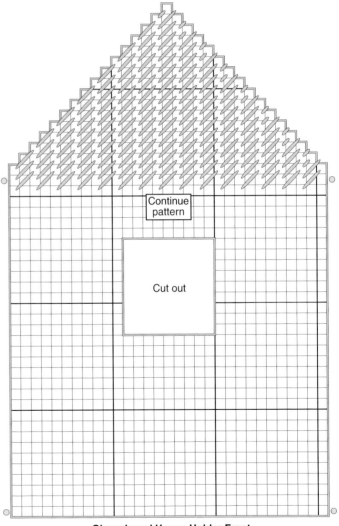

**Gingerbread House Holder Front**
31 holes x 48 holes
Cut 1

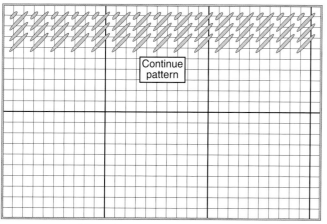

**Gingerbread House Holder Back**
31 holes x 20 holes
Cut 1

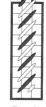

**Roof Trim**
28 holes x 28 holes
Cut 1

**Large Holly Leaf**
5 holes x 6 holes
Cut 8

**Small Holly Leaf**
3 holes x 5 holes
Cut 4

**Gingerbread House Holder Side**
13 holes x 32 holes
Cut 2, reverse 1

**Perch**
3 holes x 10 holes
Cut 2

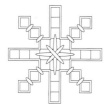

**Snowflake**
9 holes x 9 holes
Cut 3

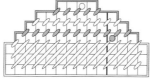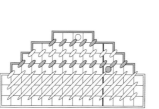

**Bluebird Hat**
14 holes x 7 holes
Cut 4

**Heart**
5 holes x 5 holes
Cut 1

**Poinsettia**
3 holes x 3 holes
Cut 5

**COLOR KEY**

| Yards | Worsted Weight Yarn |
|-------|---------------------|
| 35 (32m) | ☐ White |
| 23 (21m) | ☐ Camel |
| 20 (18.3m) | ☐ Royal blue |
| 12 (11m) | ■ Scarlet |
| 6 (5.5m) | ☐ Bright green |
| 5 (4.6m) | ☐ Bright yelllow |
| | ⟋ White Straight Stitch |
| | ⟋ Bright green Straight Stitch |
| | ⟋ Bright yellow 4-ply Straight Stitch |
| | ● Scarlet 4-ply French Knot |
| | ○ Bright yellow 2-ply French Knot |
| | ○ Attach pompom |
| | ● Attach small holly leaf |
| | ● Attach cabochon |

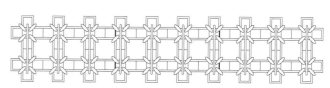

**Fence**
30 holes x 6 holes
Cut 1

# Candy Cane Holders

Designs by Debbie Tabor

**Size:** **Santa:** 5¼ inches W x 5 inches H x ⅜ inch D (13.3cm x 12.7cm x 0.9cm)
**Reindeer:** 5½ inches W x 5 inches H x ¾ inch D (14cm x 12.7cm x 1.9cm)
**Skill Level:** Beginner

## Materials

- ❏ 1 sheet clear 7-count plastic canvas
- ❏ Worsted weight yarn as listed in color key
- ❏ 6-strand cotton embroidery floss as listed in color key
- ❏ 3-inch (7.6cm) piece 3mm green chenille stem
- ❏ #18 tapestry needle
- ❏ Hot-glue gun

## Stitching Step-by-Step

### Santa

**1** Cut Santa, right and left mittens from plastic canvas according to graphs.

**2** Stitch pieces according to graphs.

**3** Using black embroidery floss through step 4, Backstitch and Straight Stitch details and work French Knot eyes. *Do not Overcast edges.*

**4** Tack mittens to matching areas of Santa between arrows.

**5** Slide candy cane between mittens; hang or display as desired.

### Reindeer

**1** Cut reindeer and two hooves from plastic canvas according to graphs.

**2** Stitch pieces according to graphs.

**3** Using black embroidery floss, Backstitch and Straight Stitch details and work French Knot eyes. Using red yarn, work French Knots on green scarf. Using white embroidery floss, Backstitch and Straight Stitch details on hooves. *Do not Overcast edges.*

**4** Using white embroidery floss, tack hooves to matching areas of reindeer between arrows.

**5** Slide candy cane between hooves; hang or display as desired.

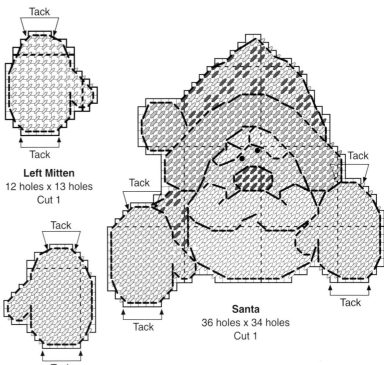

Tack

**Left Mitten**
12 holes x 13 holes
Cut 1

Tack

**Right Mitten**
12 holes x 13 holes
Cut 1

Tack

**Santa**
36 holes x 34 holes
Cut 1

## COLOR KEY

| Yards | Worsted Weight Yarn |
|---|---|
| 8 (7.3m) | ☐ Christmas green |
| 6 (5.5m) | ☐ Black |
| 4 (3.7m) | ▨ Medium clay |
| 4 (3.7m) | ☐ White |
| 3 (2.7m) | ☐ Christmas red |
| 3 (2.7m) | ▨ Eggshell |
| 3 (2.7m) | ■ Red |
| 3 (2.7m) | ☐ Taupe |
| 2 (1.8m) | ▨ Holly |
| 1 (0.9m) | ☐ Peach |
| 1 (0.9m) | ■ Pink |
| | ● Red French Knot |
| 12 (11m) | **6-Strand Embroidery Floss** |
| | ✏ Black Backstitch and Straight Stitch |
| 3 (2.7m) | ● Black French Knot |
| | ✏ White Straight Stitch |

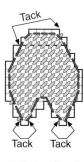

**Reindeer Hoof**
10 holes x 12 holes
Cut 2, reverse 1

Tack

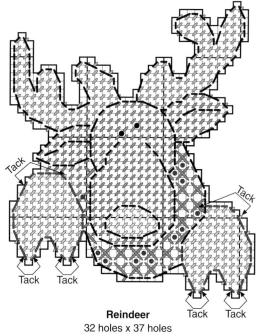

**Reindeer**
32 holes x 37 holes
Cut 1

# Boughs of Holly Place Mat

Design by Kathleen Hurley

**Size:** 4½ inches W x 7 inches H x 2 inches D
(11.4cm x 17.8cm x 5.1cm)
**Skill Level:** Beginner

## Materials

❑ Darice 18-inch (45.7cm) x 12-inch (30.5cm) white
7-count oval plastic canvas sheet
❑ Uniek Needloft plastic canvas yarn as listed in color key
❑ Uniek Needloft metallic craft cord as listed in color key
❑ #16 tapestry needle

## Stitching Step-by-Step

**1** Stitch leaves on place mat according graph, stitching twice through pairs of holes where indicated.

**2** Using Christmas red, Cross-Stitch holly berry centers first; then add small stitches over corners to complete berries.

**3** Using gold craft cord, Backstitch and Straight Stitch scrolls and other details.

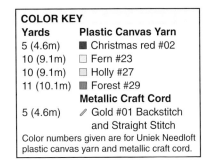

**COLOR KEY**

| Yards | Plastic Canvas Yarn |
|---|---|
| 5 (4.6m) | ■ Christmas red #02 |
| 10 (9.1m) | ☐ Fern #23 |
| 10 (9.1m) | ☐ Holly #27 |
| 11 (10.1m) | ■ Forest #29 |
| | **Metallic Craft Cord** |
| 5 (4.6m) | ⁄ Gold #01 Backstitch and Straight Stitch |

Color numbers given are for Uniek Needloft plastic canvas yarn and metallic craft cord.

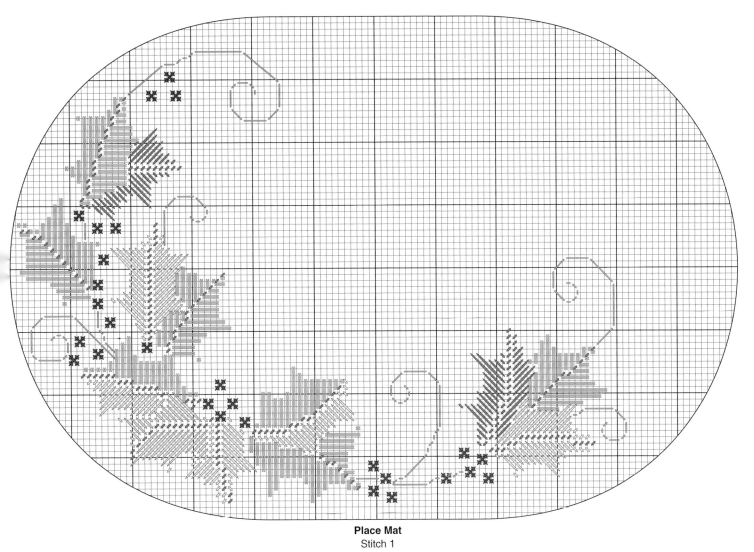

**Place Mat**
Stitch 1

# Snowy Brick Cottage

Design by Angie Arickx

**Size:** Fits regular box of tissues
**Skill Level:** Beginner

## Materials

- ❑ 1 artist-size sheet Uniek QuickCount clear 7-count plastic canvas
- ❑ Uniek Needloft plastic canvas yarn as listed in color key
- ❑ #16 tapestry needle
- ❑ Hot-glue gun

## Stitching Step-by-Step

**1** Cut cottage front and back, two cottage sides, two roof pieces, four chimney pieces, two short roof trims, two long roof trims, two trees, four large bushes and four small bushes according to graphs.

**2** Stitch pieces according to graphs, filling in uncoded areas on cottage front, back and sides with burgundy Continental Stitches, and uncoded areas on roof pieces, chimney pieces, trees and bushes with white Continental Stitches.

**3** When background stitching is complete, Straight Stitch details on chimney pieces using burgundy and work French Knot handle on door using black.

**4** Using holly and white, Overcast trees and bushes. Using white, Overcast top edges of chimney pieces. Using burgundy throughout, Whipstitch chimney pieces together along corners; Whipstitch cottage front to back and sides; Overcast top and bottom edges, except bottom edge of door, which is Overcast using camel.

**5** Using white throughout, Overcast around side and bottom edges of roof trim pieces from dot to dot. Overcast vertical edges only of chimney openings on roof sides.

**6** Referring to photo throughout, Whipstitch top edges of roof sides together, then Whipstitch bottom edges of two opposite sides of chimney to opening in roof. Bottom edges of remaining two chimney sides will not be stitched.

**7** Whipstitch top edges of long roof trims to bottom edges of roof. Whipstitch top edges of short roof trims to side edges of roof.

**8** Center and hot-glue one tree to each side of cottage. Hot-glue bushes to front and back. Hot-glue roof on cottage; feed tissues through chimney.

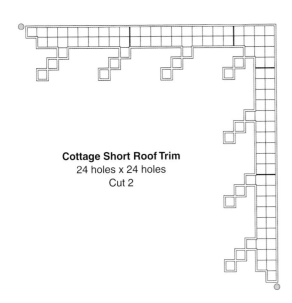

**Cottage Short Roof Trim**
24 holes x 24 holes
Cut 2

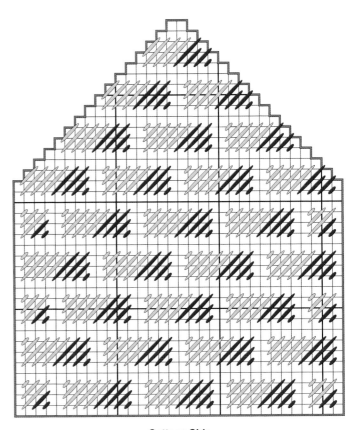

**Cottage Side**
32 holes x 37 holes
Cut 2

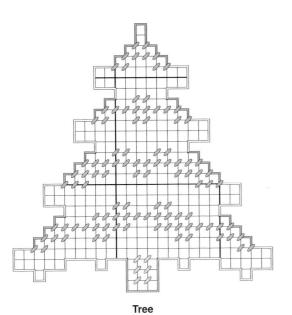

**Tree**
25 holes x 25 holes
Cut 2

| COLOR KEY | |
|---|---|
| **Yards** | **Plastic Canvas Yarn** |
| 5 (4.6m) | ■ Black #00 |
| 19 (17.4m) | ■ Red #01 |
| 25 (22.9m) | ▨ Chistmas red #02 |
| 24 (21m) | ▨ Brown #15 |
| 11 (10m) | ▨ Holly #27 |
| 53 (48.5m) | ☐ White #41 |
| 7 (6.4m) | ☐ Camel #43 |
| 33 (30.2m) | Uncoded areas on cottage front, back and sides are burgundy #03 Continental Stitches |
| | Uncoded areas on roof, chimney, tree and bushes are white #41 Continental Stitches |
| ╱ | Burgundy #03 Backstitch, Overcasting and Whipstitching |
| ● | Black #00 French Knot |

Color numbers given are for Uniek Needloft plastic canvas yarn.

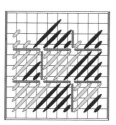

**Cottage Chimney**
10 holes x 10 holes
Cut 4

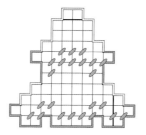

**Large Bush**
12 holes x 11 holes
Cut 4

**Small Bush**
8 holes x 6 holes
Cut 4

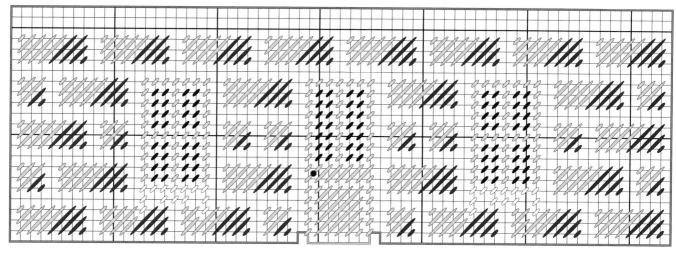

**Cottage Front & Back**
64 holes x 22 holes
Cut 2

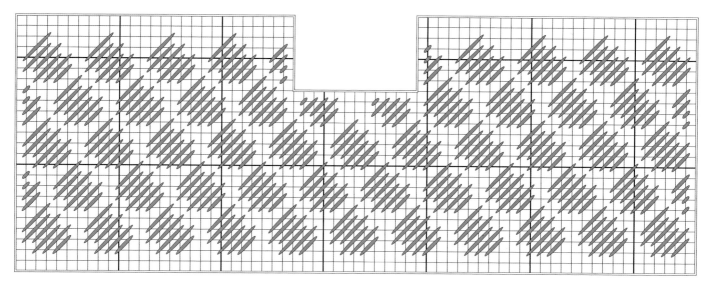

**Cottage Roof**
66 holes x 24 holes
Cut 2

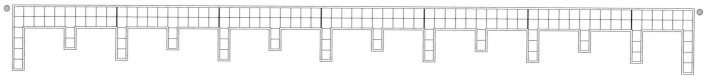

**Cottage Long Roof Trim**
66 holes x 6 holes
Cut 2

# Ho, Ho, Ho Door Decor

Design by Virginia & Michael Lamp

**Size:** 6½ inches W x 33¼ inches L
(16.5cm x 84.4cm)
**Skill Level:** Beginner

## Materials

- ❏ Artist-size sheet of clear 7-count plastic canvas
- ❏ Worsted weight yarn as listed in color key
- ❏ #16 tapestry needle
- ❏ 2 (¾-inch/19mm) gold jingle bells
- ❏ Sawtooth hanger
- ❏ Hot-glue gun

## Stitching Step-by-Step

### Santa

**1** Cut Santa head, mustache and two mittens from plastic canvas according to graphs.

**2** Stitch plastic canvas according to graphs.

**3** Overcast edges of pieces using silver for beard, hat pompom and mustache; cherry red for hat and skipper blue for mittens.

**4** Using 1 ply separated from a length of black yarn, Backstitch eyes. Using a full strand of white yarn, Straight Stitch eyebrows and hair. Using a full strand of paddy green, Straight Stitch holly leaves on hat brim. Using a full strand of cherry red yarn, work French Knot holly berries on hat brim.

### Banner

**1** Cut three H's, three O's, six holly leaves, six holly berries and one banner end from plastic canvas according to graphs. Cut also one piece 21 holes x 92 holes for banner top.

**2** Overlap bottom edge of banner top and top edge of banner end by four rows. Referring to graph for banner end, stitch entire banner in established pattern, working through both layers at overlap.

**3** Overcast edges of pieces using cornmeal for H's and O's, paddy green for banner, and matching colors for holly berries and leaves.

### Assembly

**1** Referring to photo throughout, hot-glue mustache to Santa head; hot-glue mittens to back of head, toward bottom.

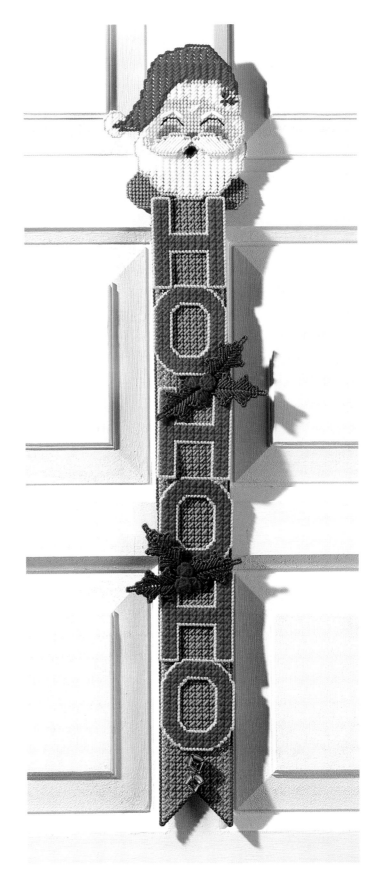

**2** Hot-glue Santa's head with mittens at banner top on right side.

**3** Hot-glue letters to spell "HO HO HO" down center of banner. Arrange holly leaves and berries in clusters and hot-glue to banner as shown.

**4** Hot-glue jingle bells at bottom of banner. Hot-glue or stitch sawtooth hanger to back of wall hanging at center top.

Overlap

**Banner End**
21 holes x 92 holes
Cut 1

**Holly Berry**
4 holes x 4 holes
Cut 6

**Holly Leaf**
9 holes x 18 holes
Cut 1

**Santa Mitten**
12 holes x 10 holes
Cut 2

**Santa Mustache**
29 holes x 6 holes
Cut 1

**Santa Head**
42 holes x 43 holes
Cut 1

**"H"**
21 holes x 25 holes
Cut 3

Cut out

**"O"**
21 holes x 25 holes
Cut 3

**COLOR KEY**

| Yards | Worsted Weight Yarn |
|---|---|
| 16 (14.6m) | □ White #1 |
| 1 (0.9m) | ■ Black #12 |
| 3 (2.7m) | Sea coral #246 |
| 6 (5.5m) | Cherry red #319 |
| 2 (1.8m) | ■ Petal pink #373 |
| 4 (3.7m) | Skipper blue #848 |
| 40 (36.6m) | ■ Hot red #390 |
| 8 (7.3m) | Silver #412 |
| 55 (50.3m) | Emerald green #676 |
| 25 (22.9m) | Paddy green #686 |
| 16 (14.6m) | □ Cornmeal #320 Overcasting |
|  | ⁄ Silver #412 Overcastaing |
|  | ⁄ White #1 Straight Stitch |
|  | ✒ Black #12 1-ply Straight Stitch |
|  | ⁄ Paddy green #686 Straight Stitch |
|  | ● Cherry red #319 French Knot |

Color numbers given are for Coats and Clark Red Heart Classic Art. E267 and Red Heart Super Saver Art. E300 worsted weight yarns.

# Rudolph's Magic

Design by Diane T. Ray

**Size:** 8 inches W x 12 inches H (20.3cm x 30.5cm)
excluding bow and greenery
**Skill Level:** Intermediate

## Materials

- ❏ 1 sheet clear 7-count plastic canvas
- ❏ Uniek Needloft plastic canvas yarn as listed in color key
- ❏ 1½ yards (1.4m) 1½-inch-wide (3.8cm) red velveteen ribbon
- ❏ Small red lightbulb
- ❏ 1½-inch-diameter musical button
- ❏ Artificial botanicals:
     Greenery bough
     Poinsettia
     Holly with pinecone/berry sprig
- ❏ #16 tapestry needle
- ❏ Sewing needle and red thread
- ❏ Hot-glue gun

## Stitching Step-by-Step

### Cutting & Stitching

**1** Cut one Rudolph according to graph, trimming out openings at nose and neck carefully.

**2** Also cut one strip 20 holes x 2 holes for nose ring, and one strip 35 holes x 3 holes for button ring.

**3** Stitch Rudolph according to graph.

**4** When background stitching is complete, Backstitch and Straight Stitch around eyes and mouth using 2 plies separated from a length of black yarn. Backstitch and Straight Stitch around ears using 2 plies separated from a length of brown yarn.

**5** Using gray, Overcast edges of antlers; using brown yarn, Overcast remaining outer edges.

**6** Bend nose ring into a circle, overlapping ends by three holes. Using red yarn through step 7, fill in nose ring with Continental Stitches; Overcast edges.

**7** Bend button ring into a circle, overlapping ends by three holes. Fill in button ring with Slanted Gobelin Stitches; Overcast edges.

## Assembly

*Note: Refer to photo throughout.*

**1** Cut ribbon into six 7-inch (17.8cm) and two 6-inch (15.2cm) pieces.

**2** *Bow:* Fold each 7-inch piece of ribbon in half. Using sewing needle and thread, stitch ends of three folded ribbons to each side of lower cutout on Rudolph.

**3** *Streamers:* Using sewing needle and thread, stitch one end of each 6-inch piece of ribbon below lower cutout on Rudolph.

**4** Insert red lightbulb into stitched nose ring; hot-glue nose ring to Rudolph at top hole. Insert music button into hole, inserting wires from front to back through lower cutout. Hot-glue button ring to Rudolph around music button.

**5** Tie or hot-glue botanicals to greenery bough as desired. Hot-glue pinecone with berry sprig to Rudolph as shown. Hot-glue assembled Rudolph to greenery; hang as desired.

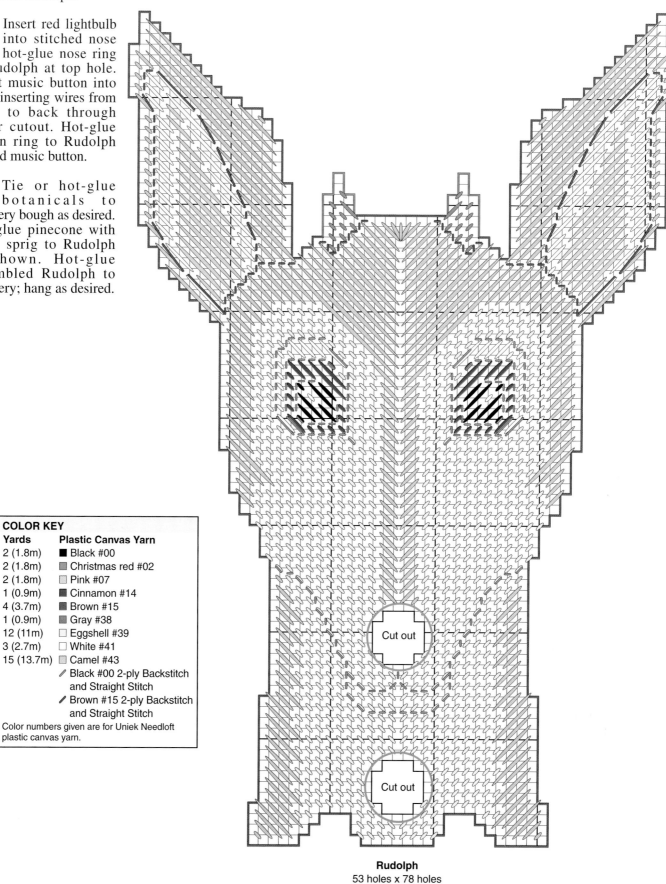

**COLOR KEY**

| Yards | Plastic Canvas Yarn |
|---|---|
| 2 (1.8m) | ■ Black #00 |
| 2 (1.8m) | Christmas red #02 |
| 2 (1.8m) | Pink #07 |
| 1 (0.9m) | Cinnamon #14 |
| 4 (3.7m) | Brown #15 |
| 1 (0.9m) | Gray #38 |
| 12 (11m) | Eggshell #39 |
| 3 (2.7m) | White #41 |
| 15 (13.7m) | Camel #43 |
| | ╱ Black #00 2-ply Backstitch and Straight Stitch |
| | ╱ Brown #15 2-ply Backstitch and Straight Stitch |

Color numbers given are for Uniek Needloft plastic canvas yarn.

Cut out

Cut out

**Rudolph**
53 holes x 78 holes
Cut 1

# Snowman for Hire

Design by Kimberly A. Suber

**Size:** 6½ inches W x 33¼ inches L
(16.5cm x 84.4cm)

**Skill Level:** Beginner

## Materials

❏ 2 sheets Uniek QuickCount clear 7-count plastic canvas
❏ Worsted weight yarn as listed in color key
❏ #16 tapestry needle
❏ Hot-glue gun

## Stitching Step-by-Step

**1** Cut snowman, sign and shovel according to graphs.

**2** Stitch pieces according to graphs, filling in uncoded areas on sign with tan Continental Stitches. Continuing pattern, work white Slanted Gobelin Stitches on body, arms and head, working partial stitches as needed to fill in completely around buttons, scarf and facial features.

**3** Overcast pieces according to graphs.

**4** When background stitching is completed, using a full strand of black throughout, Straight Stitch snowman's eyebrows and mouth and work Smyrna Cross Stitch eyes and buttons. Using 2 plies separated from a strand of black, Backstitch lettering on sign.

**5** Referring to photo, hot-glue shovel and sign to snowman's hands.

**6** Hang or display as desired.

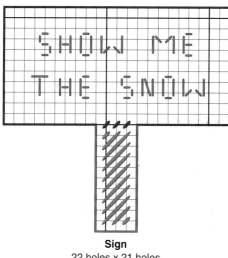

**Sign**
22 holes x 21 holes
Cut 1

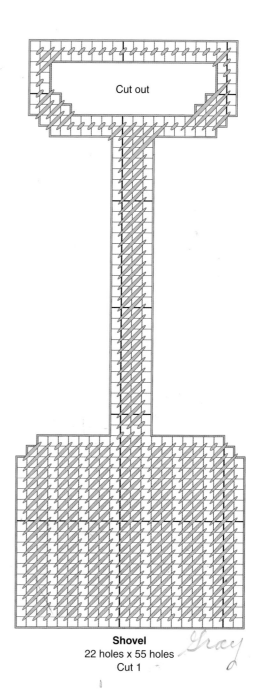

Cut out

**Shovel**
22 holes x 55 holes
Cut 1

**COLOR KEY**

| Yards | Worsted Weight Yarn |
|---|---|
| 32 (29.3m) | ☐ White |
| 6 (5.5m) | ☐ Light orange |
| 6 (5.5m) | ☐ Gray |
| 5 (4.6m) | ☐ Yellow |
| 4 (3.7m) | ☐ Bright pink |
| 4 (3.7m) | ■ Purple |
| 4 (3.7m) | ☐ Green |
| 3 (2.7m) | ☐ Turquoise |
| 2 (1.8m) | ■ Black |
| 1 (0.9m) | ☐ Bright orange |
| 1 (0.9m) | ☐ Watermelon |
| 1 (0.9m) | ☐ Brown |
| 1 (0.9m) | ■ Red |
| 3 (2.7m) | Uncoded background on sign is tan Continental Stitches |
| | ⁄ Light blue Overcasting |
| | ⁄ Black full-strand Backstitch and Straight Stitch |
| | ⁄ Black 2-ply Backstitch and Straight Stitch |

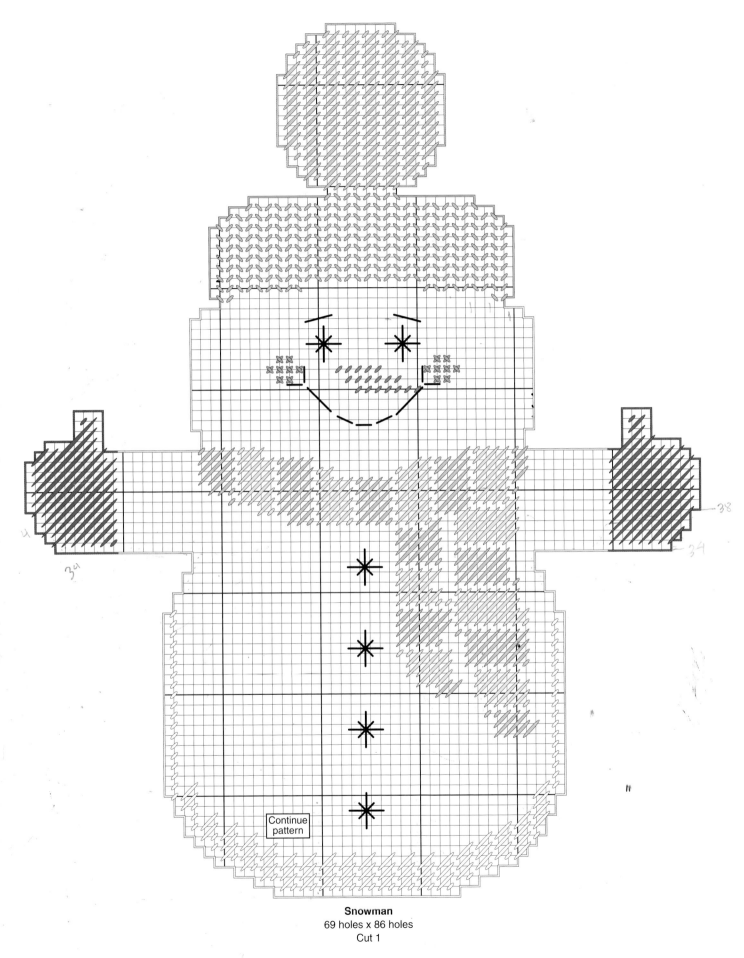

**Snowman**
69 holes x 86 holes
Cut 1

# Silent Night Nativity

Design by Alida Macor

**Size:** Fits boutique-style tissue box
**Skill Level:** Beginner

## Materials

- ❏ 1½ sheets clear 7-count plastic canvas
- ❏ Uniek Needloft plastic canvas yarn as listed in color key
- ❏ Uniek Needloft metallic craft cord as listed in color key
- ❏ #16 tapestry needle

## Stitching Step-by-Step

**1** Cut sides and top from plastic canvas according to graphs; cut out opening in top.

**2** Stitch top and sides according to graphs, working black background stitches last.

**3** Using gold/white craft cord, Overcast opening in top.

**4** Using light peach yarn throughout, Whipstitch sides together; Whipstitch assembled sides to top. Overcast bottom edges.

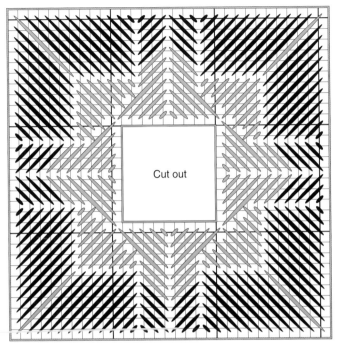

**Nativity Top**
31 holes x 31 holes
Cut 1

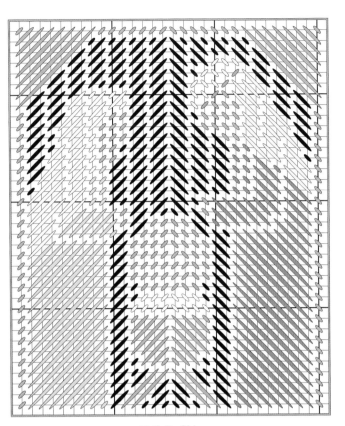

**Nativity Side**
31 holes x 37 holes
Cut 4

| COLOR KEY | |
|---|---|
| **Yards** | **Plastic Canvas Yarn** |
| 27 (24.7m) | ■ Black #00 |
| 10 (9.1m) | ■ Lavender #05 |
| 4 (3.6m) | □ Lemon #20 |
| 8 (7.3m) | ▨ Fern #23 |
| 1 (0.9m) | ■ Forest #29 |
| 7 (6.4m) | □ White #41 |
| 24 (22m) | ▨ Light peach #56 |
| | **Metallic Craft Cord** |
| 10 (9.1m) | ▨ White/gold #07 |

Color numbers given are for Uniek Needloft plastic canvas yarn and metallic craft cord.

306 E. Parr Road
Berne, IN 46711
www.NeedlecraftShop.com
© 2006 The Needlecraft Shop

The full line of The Needlecraft Shop
products is carried by Annie's Attic catalog.
**TOLL-FREE ORDER LINE**
or to request a free catalog
(800) 582-6643
**Customer Service**
(800) 449-0440
**Fax (800) 882-6643**
Visit www.AnniesAttic.com

ISBN: 978-1-57367-230-6

## Getting Started

### Before You Cut

Buy one brand of canvas for each entire project, as brands can differ slightly in the distance between bars. Count holes carefully from the graph before you cut, using the bolder lines that show each 10 holes. These 10-mesh lines begin in the lower left corner of each graph to make counting easier. Mark canvas before cutting, then remove all marks completely before stitching. If the piece is cut in a rectangular or square shape and is either not worked, or worked with only one color and one type of stitch, we do not include the graph in the pattern. Instead, we give the cutting and stitching instructions in the general instructions or with the individual project instructions.

### Covering the Canvas

Bring needle up from back of work, leaving a short length of yarn on back of canvas; work over short length to secure. To end a thread, weave needle and thread through the wrong side of your last few stitches; clip. Follow the numbers on the small graphs beside each stitch illustration; bring your needle up from the back of the work on odd numbers and down through the front of the work on even numbers. Work embroidery stitches last, after the canvas has been completely covered by the needlepoint stitches.

## Shopping for Supplies

For supplies, first shop your local craft and needlework stores. Some supplies may be found in fabric, hardware and discount stores. If you are unable to find the supplies you need, please call Annie's Attic at (800) 259-4000 to request a free catalog that sells plastic canvas supplies.

## Basic Stitches

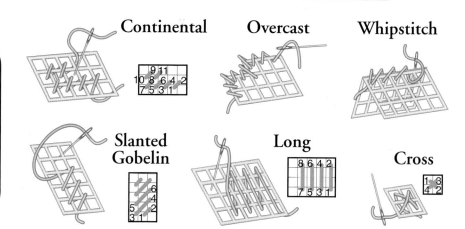

## Embroidery Stitches

### French Knot
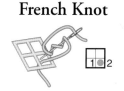

### Lazy Daisy

### Backstitch

### Straight
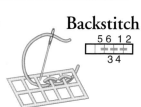

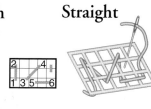

**METRIC KEY:**
millimeters = (mm)
centimeters = (cm)
meters = (m)
grams = (g)